Bazaar Cookb

The Bazaar Cookbook

BBC BOOKS

The recipe on page 112 is reproduced
with the kind permission of Thorsons
Publishers Ltd.

Page design: Chris Bell
Illustrations: Juliet Breese
Cover photographs: main picture;
Lesley Waters © BBC; clockwise from
top right; Kevin Woodford © HUW
DAVIES; Lynda Brown © DAVID HYDE;
Phil Diamond © TODAY NEWS (UK)
LTD; Shirley Goode © BBC;
Sophie Grigson © SWINDON EVENING
ADVERTISER; Gill MacLennan
© WOMAN MAGAZINE.

Published by BBC Books,
A division of BBC Enterprises Ltd,
Woodlands, 80 Wood Lane, London
W12 0TT

This book is set in 11/12 pt Palatino
Typeset and printed in England by
Redwood Burn Ltd, Trowbridge,
Wiltshire

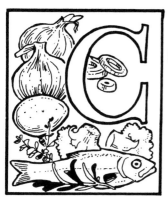

ontents

Introduction

One of the chief pleasures of the last two series of *Bazaar* has been meeting and getting to know a wide variety of talented cooks who can conjure up an appetising meal as if by magic. Not all of us have that gift but whether we're feeding a family or just ourselves, we want our meals to be filling, nutritious and tasty. Our cooks showed us how to do this and they've included many of their great ideas in this book.

From Shirley Goode and Lynda Brown we discovered the gentle art of budgeting. My heart always used to sink at the very word 'budgeting', but, believe me, Shirley and Lynda can turn it into a challenge which makes shopping and cooking sizzle with excitement. The price of feeding a family can sometimes be overwhelming. The weekly amount spent on food seems like the national debt. But Shirley and Lynda showed us how to find out how much our meals *really* cost. You may know how much money you set aside each week for food, but do you know how much you spent on last Wednesday's supper? When you've got a few minutes to spare, work out how much the meals you make regularly really cost. When you've twigged which are the inexpensive ingredients, use them regularly – for example, a meal based on pancakes (made with flour which is cheap) can be filling *and* imaginative. You only need to do this once or twice to understand the true cost of food. And the other tip Shirley and Lynda emphasised was to have a good storecupboard – and to *use* it. Once you've found out the value of your own food, you'll think twice about going out and buying a packet of biscuits when you know you can make twice as many for half the price yourself.

Another delight of the series was meeting fishmonger Phil Diamond and listening to him enthusing about his favourite food – fish, of course! Get to know your fishmonger. As Phil said, he'll help you sort out the cod from the coley, the haddock from the hake and do all those off-putting jobs like gutting and beheading. So what we take home is the original fast food – a tasty meal in minutes.

Simple sophistication was Sophie Grigson's message – interesting food doesn't have to be complicated or fussy. Gill MacLennan showed us how to beat the take-aways at their own game and Kevin Woodford provided enough enthusiasm to fire the imaginations of the most reluctant of cooks! Then take the humble spud – not the most glamorous vegetable is it, not something you'd go specially to the Ritz to eat. But in the hands of Lesley Waters, all I can say is that it's pure magic. Her recipe for spicy potato skins has become known simply as *Bazaar* potatoes among the production team.

On top of the pleasure of watching all our cooks at work, came the enormous privilege of hearing from and sometimes meeting *Bazaar* viewers, without whom, as they say, none of this would have been possible. So my thanks to everyone who took the trouble to send in their recipe ideas and I hope you enjoy the ones we have included here. But above all, I'd like to say a special thank you to Carol Smith whose family faced a difficult period of unemployment with courage, determination and, remarkably, without losing their sense of fun. She was an inspiration to us all on *Bazaar* and I hope to those of you who saw her on the programmes.

This book is dedicated to *Bazaar* viewers who, like Carol, may be struggling through difficult times. You may feel some of the recipes sound too expensive and it's true that some aren't exactly *cheap* (we all have to have treats sometimes). But just remember Shirley's secret – once you've found out the true value of your own food, what once seemed a luxury could now be on your plate for supper.

So, happy cooking and do let me know how you get on.

Erica Griffiths
Producer, *Bazaar*

oups and starters

Tomato soup de luxe

Serves 4

This is a lovely soup which is equally good served hot during winter or chilled for a summer lunch. It is well worth preparing in bulk to freeze, ready for unexpected guests.

Shirley Goode

1 × 14 oz (397 g) can plum tomatoes
3 oz (75 g) dried apricots, coarsely chopped
15 fl oz (450 ml) chicken stock
2 teaspoons sugar
2 rounded teaspoons tomato purée
Salt and freshly ground black pepper
A little whipping cream or top of the milk

Strain the can of tomatoes through a sieve, rubbing the flesh through with a wooden spoon. Discard the seeds. Stir the apricots into the tomatoes and leave to soak overnight.

Next day, put tomato and apricots into a saucepan with the stock, sugar and tomato purée, and simmer for 20 minutes. Cool slightly, then purée the mixture in a blender or processor. (For a really smooth soup continue with a firm rub through a sieve.) Re-heat to boiling and season to taste. Ladle into individual bowls and swirl a little cream, if using, in each just before serving.

Tomato and red pepper soup

Serves 4

Without doubt, the two best herbs to use in this soup are basil or coriander, but they do have to be fresh – dried basil is barely even a vague approximation to the real thing. Marjoram is not bad, again preferably fresh, but if you have to use dried, add only ¹/₄ teaspoon with the tomatoes, and stir fresh parsley in at the end. In the summer this soup is wonderful served lightly chilled – use oil rather than butter which might congeal. Serve with good crusty bread.

Sophie Grigson

2 tablespoons
  sunflower oil
1 onion, chopped
2 garlic cloves, chopped
2 red peppers, de-
  seeded and chopped
1½ lb (750 g) tomatoes,
  skinned, de-seeded
  and coarsely
  chopped
¾ pint (450 ml) chicken
  stock or water
1 teaspoon sugar
1 teaspoon red wine
  vinegar
Salt and freshly ground
  black pepper
Fresh coriander, basil
  or marjoram

Heat the oil in a large saucepan and add the onion, garlic and peppers. Cook gently until softened. Add the tomatoes, 4 fl oz (120 ml) of the stock, sugar, vinegar, a little salt and pepper and about 10 coriander or basil sprigs or 2 marjoram sprigs. Bring to the boil, reduce heat to a simmer and cook for 20–30 minutes.

Pick out the herbs. Purée the soup in a blender or food processor, then stir in the remaining stock. Re-heat and adjust the seasoning.

Tear about 2 tablespoonfuls of basil or coriander leaves, or chop 1 tablespoon fresh marjoram leaves, and stir into the soup. Ladle into individual bowls and serve hot.

Pea pod soup

Serves 4

The sweet flesh of plump and juicy pea pods makes a very good soup as easily as . . . shelling peas!

Shirley Goode

1½ lb (750 g) pea pods,
  topped, tailed,
  trimmed and
  coarsely chopped
A few extra peas
Knob of concentrated
  butter (see opposite)
1 large onion, chopped
1½ pints (900 ml)
  chicken stock
Top of the milk or
  single cream
Salt and freshly ground
  black pepper
Croûtons, to garnish

Put the pea pods in a saucepan with a few peas and enough water to cover. Bring to the boil, reduce heat to a simmer and cook for about 15 minutes. Drain well, then purée in a blender or food processor. Alternatively, rub the pods through a sieve.

Melt the butter in a large saucepan, add the onion and fry until softened but not browned. Add the pea purée and the stock, and heat until just simmering. Stir in a little milk or cream, and season to taste. Ladle into individual bowls and sprinkle croûtons over the tops. Serve hot.

Marrow and ginger soup

One very good way to use up inexpensive vegetable marrow is to make this soup. It becomes even more economical with the use of concentrated butter, giving a luxury flavour at less than the cost of margarine. (Concentrated butter is butter that has had most of its water and salt removed. Because it is subsidised by the EEC it is substantially less expensive than ordinary butter.)

Shirley Goode

1 oz (25 g) concentrated butter
1 teaspoon ground ginger
¹/₂ teaspoon ground cinnamon
1 onion, chopped
1 lb (450 g) marrow, peeled and cut into small chunks
1 pint (600 ml) chicken stock
Salt and freshly ground black pepper
2 fl oz (50 ml) single cream or top of the milk

Melt the butter in a large saucepan and add the ginger, cinnamon and the onion. Gently fry for a few minutes until the onion is softened but not coloured. Add the marrow and fry for a further 2 minutes.

Pour in the stock, reduce the heat to a simmer, cover and simmer until the marrow is tender (about 15 minutes, depending on the ripeness of the marrow). Remove from heat and set aside for a few minutes, then purée in a blender or food processor (you will need to do this in two batches). Return to the pan, season to taste and stir in the cream or milk. Re-heat gently but do not boil. Ladle into individual bowls and serve hot.

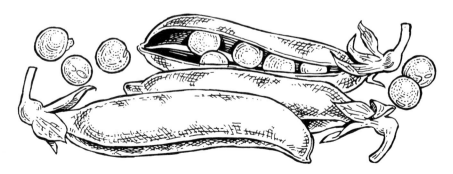

Cream of broccoli soup with croûtons

Serves 4

Some of my favourite soups I owe to my friend, Norma Simons. This is one of them. Broccoli is usually at its cheapest from November to February.

Phil Diamond

1 ½ lb (750 g) broccoli, trimmed
2 chicken stock cubes, crushed
1 tablespoon cornflour
10 fl oz (300 ml) fromage frais, or natural yoghurt
Salt and freshly ground black pepper
2 oz (50 g) croûtons, to garnish

Cook the broccoli in 1½ pints (900 ml) of water until tender. Strain the broccoli, reserving the cooking liquid. Purée the broccoli in a blender or food processor, then return to the saucepan with the cooking liquid, adding the stock cubes. Bring to the boil for 1 minute, then reduce heat to a simmer. Blend the cornflour with a little water to make a smooth paste. Gradually stir the cornflour paste and fromage frais or yoghurt into the soup, and continue simmering for 2–3 minutes, stirring frequently. Season to taste. Ladle into individual bowls and garnish with croûtons. Serve hot.

Cream of mackerel soup

Serves 4

This soup tastes much richer and luxurious than it actually is. In fact, it serves four for less than £1.50, including a loaf of home-made bread (see page 112).

Bernadine Lawrence, London

2 onions, finely chopped
1 carrot, grated
2 garlic cloves, crushed
2 tablespoons sunflower oil
1 mackerel fillet
2 oz (50 g) mushrooms, roughly chopped
1 small bunch parsley, finely chopped

Gently sauté the onions, carrots and garlic in the oil until soft but not brown. Add the mackerel fillet, left whole, with the mushrooms and parsley. Sauté for a further 5 minutes until the fish turns flaky and opaque. You can cover the pan to speed up the cooking time.

Meanwhile, make the base for the soup. Put the flour in a large saucepan and add the milk very gradually,

3 oz (75 g) flour
1¹/₂ pints (900 ml) milk
Salt and pepper
Watercress, to garnish
(optional)

stirring all the time with a wooden spoon until the flour is smoothly blended. Bring to the boil slowly, still stirring, then turn down the heat and stir until thick.

Add the sautéed vegetables and fish. If the skin is still attached to the fish, flake the fish into the soup and discard the skin. The fish should flake further as you stir. Season the soup to taste and add 4 fl oz (120 ml) water to thin it down. Garnish with watercress, if you wish, and serve with warm crusty bread.

Cream of chicken, celery and Stilton soup
Serves 4

This soup is, for me, the epitome of good English ingredients that complement each other perfectly. The Stilton will keep your guests guessing as to what the delicious mystery flavour enhancing the celery is.

Kevin Woodford

2 oz (50 g) sunflower margarine
4 oz (100 g) onion, sliced
4 oz (100 g) leek, sliced and well rinsed
7 oz (200 g) celery, sliced
2 oz (50 g) plain flour
1³/₄ pint (1 litre) hot chicken stock
2 oz (50 g) Stilton cheese, crumbled
4 fl oz (120 ml) top of the milk
Salt and freshly ground black pepper

Melt the margarine in a large saucepan. Add the vegetables and cook until softened but not coloured. Stir in the flour and slowly cook for 2–3 minutes without colouring. Cool slightly.

Gradually stir in the hot stock. Bring to the boil, then reduce heat to a simmer, cover and cook for 45 minutes, skimming the surface as necessary. Pass through a strainer or purée in a blender or food processor. Return to the pan and bring back to the boil. Add the Stilton and milk, stirring until the cheese melts. Season to taste with salt and pepper. Ladle into individual bowls and serve hot.

Vegetable chowder

Serves 4

A chowder is a thick, main-course soup. The basic ingredients are the potatoes, onions, carrots and bacon, and once you've got those you can add whatever vegetables are in season. A small can of drained and flaked tuna or some diced smoked haddock can be added at the end of cooking.

Sophie Grigson

1 tablespoon sunflower oil
1 onion, chopped
4 bacon rashers, rinded and cut into strips
2 carrots, scraped and cut into ½ in (1 cm) chunks
1 large potato, peeled and cut into ½ in (1 cm) cubes
2 tablespoons plain flour
1½–2 pints (900 ml–1.2 litres) milk
1 bay leaf
¼ teaspoon dried thyme
Salt and freshly ground black pepper
2 oz (50 g) frozen peas or sweetcorn, thawed
2 hard-boiled eggs, finely chopped
Grated cheese, to serve

Heat the oil in a large saucepan. Add the onion and cook, stirring, until softened but not brown. Add the bacon and stir until just cooked. Add the carrots and potato and stir to coat well in the oil. Sprinkle the flour on the vegetables, then stir for a further minute so it is evenly distributed. Add the milk, herbs and salt and pepper to taste. Bring to the boil, reduce heat to a simmer and cook for 10 minutes. Add the peas and continue simmering until all vegetables are cooked. Adjust the seasonings. Put the eggs and cheese into separate small bowls and pass around, when serving the soup, so each person can sprinkle a little over their soup.

Bazaar Viewer's Tip
A large potato, finely grated and stirred into a thin broth, will immediately thicken it and provide a filling soup.

Cabbage and potato soup

Serves 4

Based on the Portuguese soup caldo verde, *nothing could be simpler to make or tastier than this. The base, a simple potato and onion broth, can be used for a number of potato soups and is worth making in quantity to freeze. Similarly, you can make the soup with any kind of green cabbage; if you are a gardener, Swiss chard is almost worth growing for this soup alone.*

A variation I make often at home is the Italian version: thin the soup with water and dribble over some olive oil into each bowl before serving.

Half the success of this soup is shredding the cabbage as finely as you can. The best way to do this is to roll the leaves up tightly like a sausage or cigar, then slice downwards with a serrated knife, shaving off thin strips. This way the cabbage needs hardly any cooking and keeps deliciously crisp and green in the soup.

Lynda Brown

8 oz (225 g) potatoes, peeled and coarsely chopped
1 small onion, coarsely chopped
2 oz (50 g) streaky bacon rashers, rinded, or bacon bits, cut into small strips
2–3 oz (50–75 g) outer cabbage leaves, very finely shredded
About 5 fl oz (150 ml) milk, or milk and water mixed

Place the potatoes and onions in a saucepan with 15 fl oz (450 ml) water. Cover, bring to the boil, then reduce the heat and cook for about 20 minutes until soft. Purée in a blender or food processor until smooth, then return to the pan.

Meanwhile, place the bacon in a frying-pan and fry in its own fat until crisp.

Add the cabbage to the soup with enough milk, or milk and water, to give the desired consistency, then cook for a couple of minutes just until the cabbage has wilted. Stir in the bacon and its fat. Ladle into individual bowls and serve hot.

17

Apple and cheese soup with herb dumplings

This soup is a meal in itself!

Lesley Waters

Serves 4

2 oz (50 g) butter
1 onion, finely chopped
1 garlic clove, crushed
1½ oz (40 g) plain flour
4 fl oz (120 ml) dry cider or white wine (optional)
1½ pints (900 ml) vegetable or chicken stock
1 large bay leaf
2 eating apples, peeled, cored and finely diced
10 oz (275 g) mature Cheddar cheese, grated
2 tablespoons single cream or top of the milk
Salt and freshly ground black pepper
Finely chopped fresh parsley, to garnish
Herb dumplings
4 oz (100 g) plain flour
A good pinch of salt
1 teaspoon baking powder
2 oz (50 g) shredded suet
1 tablespoon chopped fresh parsley
1 teaspoon dried thyme
Grated zest of 1 lemon

Melt the butter in a large saucepan, then add the onion and garlic and cook until softened but not coloured. Add the flour and cook for 30 seconds. Remove from the heat and stir in the cider or wine, stock and bay leaf, stirring until smooth. (If you are not using any alcohol, increase the stock by 4 fl oz.) Return to the heat and slowly bring to the boil, stirring constantly, until the soup thickens. Reduce the heat to a simmer and cook for 15 minutes, then add the apples and continue simmering for a further 20 minutes. Remove from the heat and stir in the grated cheese. Add the cream or milk and season to taste with salt and pepper; the consistency should be like thin cream.

To make the dumplings, sieve the flour, salt and baking powder together, then mix in the suet, herbs, grated lemon zest and just enough water to form a slightly sticky dough. Roll the dough into little balls (about 8) with floured hands. Add the dumplings to the soup, cover and simmer for a further 15 minutes. Ladle into individual bowls and garnish with parsley. Serve hot.

Lentil winter warmer

Serves 4

I sometimes wonder what we would do without lentils. They make marvellous simple and nourishing soups, and are no trouble to cook, requiring no soaking. They tend to be dusty, so you need to rinse them first and to check for any pieces of grit, but that is all.

This is another good soup to make in quantity and store in the freezer. Served with bread and perhaps an apple to follow, and you have a good sustaining lunch for hardly any effort or cost to speak of.

Lynda Brown

A knob of butter, or a little sunflower oil
1 carrot, peeled and finely chopped
½ onion, finely chopped
4 oz (100 g) split red lentils, rinsed and picked over
1 dessertspoon tomato purée, or 1–2 squashy frying tomatoes
1 bay leaf
Salt

Melt the butter or heat the oil in a saucepan. Add the carrot and onion and cook over a gentle heat until softened. Add the remaining ingredients and 1 pint (600 ml) water, cover and cook about 20 minutes until the lentils are soft.

Remove the bay leaf and blend two thirds of the soup in a blender or food processor until smooth. Return to the pan and mix well with the remaining soup. Return to the boil and season to taste with salt if you wish. If necessary, dilute with a little extra water or milk. Ladle into individual bowls and serve hot.

19

Scots broth

Serves 8

Make this soup as thick and hearty or as clear as you wish but be sure you use good lamb stock and fresh root vegetables, and, of course, lots of barley. Served with some oatcakes (page 114) or a hunk of buttered wholemeal bread, it's a meal in a bowl.

Gill MacLennan

2 lb (1 kg) scrag-end neck of lamb
1 onion, chopped
1 small swede, thickly peeled and diced
2 large carrots, scraped and diced
1 leek, chopped and well rinsed
4 oz (100 g) pearl barley
4 oz (100 g) curly kale or spring greens, washed and finely shredded
Salt and freshly ground black pepper
Chopped fresh parsley, to serve

Place the lamb in a pan with 3½ pints (2 litres) water. Bring to the boil, reduce heat to a simmer, cover and cook for 2 hours.

Strain off the stock into a large bowl, set aside to cool, then chill until the fat sets in a hard creamy layer on top. Remove and discard the fat. Place the stock, which will be a jelly, in a large pan.

Cut the lamb into small chunks and add to the pan with the onion, swede, carrots, leek and barley. Bring to the boil, reduce heat to a simmer, cover and cook for 1 hour.

Add the kale and boil for 1 minute only. Add salt and pepper to taste, and sprinkle generously with parsley just before serving. Ladle into individual bowls and serve hot.

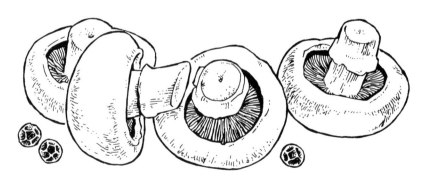

Housewife's pâté

Serves 4–6

Recipes for pâtés are often daunting and rather grand, which, I suspect, puts people off trying to make them. This is a great pity, for many are good homely dishes, which are easily made, adapt well to ingredients at hand and which are considerably cheaper than the bought varieties. This one, for example, costs around 45p – the price you'd pay for a quarter of the amount from a supermarket.

Pork back fat can come from bacon or pork chops – or, maybe, cadged from the butcher for nothing.

Lynda Brown

4 oz (100 g) pig's liver
2 oz (50 g) pork back fat, cubed
4 oz (100 g) fresh wholemeal or white breadcrumbs, soaked in 5 fl oz (150 ml) milk
1 small egg
1 in (2.5 cm) piece of carrot, peeled and finely grated
1 teaspoon minced onion
1 heaped tablespoon finely chopped mushrooms
¹/₄ teaspoon *each* grated nutmeg, thyme, black pepper and crumbled or powdered bay leaf
¹/₂ teaspoon salt
1 tablespoon brandy (optional)

Mince the liver and the fat, either with a mincer or in a food processor, putting in the fat first, then adding the liver. Give it short bursts and be careful not to process to a slush. Transfer to a bowl, add the remaining ingredients and beat well; the mixture rather resembles a thick plum pudding batter. Set the mixture aside for a couple of hours for the flavours to blend.

Pre-heat the oven to gas mark 1, 275°F (140°C).

Pour into a deep ovenproof dish, leaving 1 in (2.5 cm) headspace. Set this dish in a roasting pan, or large ovenproof dish, containing 1 in (2.5 cm) cold water. Cook for about 1¹/₂ hours or until the pâté shrinks slightly from the sides and the juices run clear when a skewer is inserted.

Set aside to cool, then leave for 24 hours before serving. It keeps for a few days in the refrigerator but like all pâtés it does not freeze well.

Chicken liver pâté with orange and coriander

Serves 4

Chicken liver pâté is one of the simplest and most successful of all pâtés to make. If you don't have time to roast the coriander seeds and flavour the butter with them, leave them out altogether, and instead add the grated zest of half the orange. You can also layer the pâté with strips of grilled and skinned red pepper to give extra flavour.

Sophie Grigson

1 teaspoon coriander seeds
2 oz (50 g) butter
8 oz (225 g) chicken livers, trimmed and quartered
Pinch of dried thyme
2 tablespoons orange juice
Salt and freshly ground black pepper
Hot toast, to serve

Heat a small heavy-based pan, then add the coriander seeds and shake the pan gently until the seeds turn a shade darker. Remove the seeds from the pan and crush lightly. Melt the butter with the seeds, and infuse over the lowest possible heat for 10 minutes. Strain well, discarding the seeds.

Sauté the livers in the coriander-flavoured butter for a few minutes with the thyme, until just cooked but still pink in the centres.

Purée the livers in a blender or food processor, or mash, with their butter, the orange juice and salt and pepper to taste. Pack into a small pot, cover and chill in the fridge until firm. Make wavy patterns on the top with the tines of a fork. Serve cold with hot toast.

Wholemeal blinis with ham and garlic sauce

Makes 15

These tasty Russian pancakes can be served with a variety of different fillings. Hummus and taramasalata make an excellent alternative to the ham and garlic sauce.

Lesley Waters

4 oz (100 g) plain wholemeal flour
4 oz (100 g) granary or unbleached flour
Pinch of salt
2 tablespoons sesame seeds
¹/₂ oz (15 g) fresh yeast, or ¹/₄ oz (7 g) dried
Pinch of sugar
10 fl oz (300 ml) warm milk
2 eggs, separated
1 tablespoon oil
Sauce
10 fl oz (300 ml) sour cream or thick Greek yoghurt
4 oz (100 g) cooked ham, cut into thin strips
1 garlic clove, crushed
2 tablespoons finely chopped fresh parsley
Salt and freshly ground black pepper

Sift the 2 flours into a large mixing bowl with the salt, then stir in the sesame seeds. In a smaller bowl, cream the fresh yeast and sugar together, add the warm milk and egg yolks and mix together until smooth. If using dried yeast, mix with the sugar and milk and set aside for 10–15 minutes until frothy.

Pour the yeast mixture into the flours and mix together. Cover and leave in a warm place for 1 hour.

Meanwhile, make the sauce. Combine all the ingredients and stir well together. Season to taste with salt and pepper.

When the yeast batter has risen, beat the egg whites until stiff, then fold into the batter with a large metal spoon. Heat a frying-pan, then add the oil. Drop large spoonfuls of the batter into the pan and cook for about 1 minute on each side until lightly browned. Cook in batches until all the batter is used. Keep the cooked blinis warm.

Spread the blinis with the sauce and arrange on a large warm plate, or stack the blinis, sandwiched with the sauce. Serve at once.

Vegetable terrine with tomato and thyme purée

Serves 4

When you're making this multi-layered terrine, make sure that the spinach and vegetable purées have been slightly dried out over heat to evaporate excess water.

Lesley Waters

Sunflower oil
8 eggs, beaten
2 oz (50 g) cooked
 spinach
1 garlic clove, crushed
Grated nutmeg
Salt and freshly ground
 black pepper
8 oz (225 g) carrots,
 cooked and puréed
8 oz (225 g) broccoli,
 cooked and puréed
2 oz (50 g) Cheddar
 cheese, grated
1 tablespoon finely
 chopped fresh
 parsley
*Tomato and thyme
 purée*
1 tablespoon chopped
 fresh thyme
2 tomatoes, chopped
2 tablespoons
 sunflower oil
Squeeze of lemon juice
Salt and freshly ground
 black pepper

Pre-heat the oven to gas mark 3, 325°F (160°C). Brush a 1 lb (500 g) loaf tin with a little oil and place a piece of greased greaseproof paper or aluminium foil on the base.

 Take 4 mixing bowls, put 2 eggs in each and beat them. Add the spinach, garlic, nutmeg and salt and pepper to taste to 1 bowl and mix well. Pour this mixture into the prepared tin, cover with aluminium foil and place in a roasting tin with enough boiling water to come half-way up the loaf tin. Bake for 10–15 minutes or until firm. minutes or until firm.

 Meanwhile, prepare the other fillings. Place the carrot purée in the second bowl, the broccoli purée in the third bowl and the cheese and the parsley in fourth bowl. Beat each filling until smooth and season to taste with salt and pepper.

 When the spinach layer is cooked, pour on the carrot mixture. Cover with the foil and cook again 10–15 minutes or until firm. Continue with the remaining fillings, until the 4 layers are set.

 Remove the terrine from the oven and set aside to cool for 10 minutes.

 Meanwhile, make the tomato and thyme purée. Put all the ingredients in a blender or food processor and purée until very smooth. Season to taste with salt and pepper.

To serve, slice the warm vegetable terrine into thick slices and arrange on a serving plate, accompanied by the tomato and thyme purée.

Aubergine dip

Serves 4–6

I remember my father preparing this dish when I was a young boy, and it has always been special to me. Look out for aubergines that are slightly over-ripe and so marked down. They are usually at their cheapest in September.

Phil Diamond

2 lb (1 kg) medium-sized aubergines
2 tablespoons sunflower oil
Salt and freshly ground black pepper
2 tomatoes, cut into wedges
2 oz (50 g) black olives

Pre-heat the grill to high.

Prick aubergines all over with a fork, then place under the grill and cook until skin just starts to burn. Using tongs turn the aubergines a quarter turn and char again. Repeat charring and turning the aubergines until the whole skin is blistered. Remove from the grill and set aside to cool for 10 minutes.

Split the aubergines lengthways and scoop out the flesh into a colander and leave for 30 minutes to drain.

Purée the drained flesh in a blender or a food processor for 1¹/₂ minutes, adding the sunflower oil and salt and pepper to taste. Place the mixture in a serving dish and garnish with black olives and tomatoes, or spoon into ramekins and garnish. Chill until ready to serve.

Smoked fish and horseradish mousse

Serves 4–6 as a starter

The lovely thing about this recipe is the openness of the main ingredient. If you are feeling flush or intent on producing a seduction meal, then you can splash out on salmon. If an earthy economical dish is the order of the day, then use mackerel. The choice is yours!

Kevin Woodford

1 teaspoon gelatine
1 small eating apple, peeled, cored and cooked
Juice of ½ lemon
6 oz (175 g) smoked fish, skinned and flaked
½ teaspoon horse-radish cream
Salt and freshly ground black pepper
2½ fl oz (65 ml) double cream
1 egg white
4–6 lemon slices, to garnish
4–6 small fresh mint leaves, to garnish
Pinch of paprika, to garnish
Brown bread, to serve

Sprinkle the gelatine over 2 fl oz (50 ml) cold water in a small saucepan and dissolve, gently heating and stirring the mixture until it becomes clear. Stir in the apple and lemon juice.

Place the fish and the horseradish cream in a blender or food processor and process until smooth. Season with salt and black pepper. Mix well with the apple mixture.

Whip the cream until lightly thickened. In a separate bowl, whip the egg white until stiff. Gently fold in the cream with a large metal spoon, then the egg white. Divide into ramekins and place in the refrigerator to set and chill until ready to serve.

Serve each garnished with a slice of lemon, mint leaf and a very light dusting of paprika, accompanied by buttered brown bread.

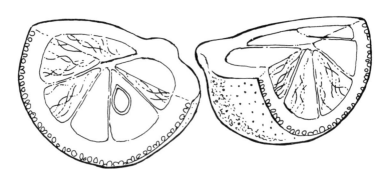

Carrot soufflé

Serves 4

Don't be put off by the word soufflé; it can sound a little grand, when, in fact, it is an inexpensive, simple dish. You can use parsnip or turnip instead of carrot.

Lesley Waters

1 tablespoon finely grated Cheddar or Parmesan cheese
1 lb (450 g) carrots, thinly sliced
10 fl oz (300 ml) milk
1 tablespoon turmeric
Salt and freshly ground black pepper
2 oz (50 g) butter
2 oz (50 g) plain flour
4 eggs, separated
2 tablespoons chopped fresh parsley
1 extra egg white

Pre-heat the oven to gas mark 6, 400°F (200°C).

Grease a 2½ pint (1.5 litre) soufflé dish or cake tin. Tip in the cheese and turn the dish about so the sides and base are evenly coated, reserving the excess cheese.

Place the carrots in a saucepan with the milk, turmeric and a pinch of salt. Cook over medium heat until the carrots are tender. Purée in a blender or food processor until smooth.

Melt the butter in a medium-sized saucepan. Stir in the flour and cook for 30 seconds. Remove from the heat and stir in the carrot mixture. Beat until very smooth, then return to the heat and bring to the boil, stirring constantly, for about 3 minutes until very thick and smooth. Remove from the heat and beat in the egg yolks and parsley and season to taste. (The flavour should be quite strong, as the egg whites will dilute the taste.)

Whisk the egg whites until stiff and fold half into the carrot mixture quite quickly with a large metal spoon. Add the remaining whites and fold in very gently. Spoon into the prepared soufflé dish and sprinkle the remaining cheese over the top. Cook for 30 minutes. Serve at once.

Spicy potato skins with garlic sauce

Serves 4

These potato skins are really delicious. They can be served as a first course or as a main supper dish, accompanied by a crisp green salad.

Lesley Waters

1 lb (450 g) washed potato peelings
2 teaspoons Tabasco sauce
4 tablespoons dark soy sauce
1 tablespoon paprika
2 tablespoons sunflower oil
Salt and freshly ground black pepper
Garlic sauce
10 fl oz (300 ml) natural yoghurt
1 large garlic clove, crushed
Grated nutmeg

Pre-heat the oven to gas mark 7, 425°F (220°C).

Mix together the Tabasco, soy sauce, paprika, sunflower oil and salt and pepper to taste in a large bowl. Toss the potato peelings in this mixture.

Tip the coated skins into a roasting tin, spread them out and bake for 30 minutes until golden brown and very crisp.

Meanwhile, make the garlic sauce. Mix together the yoghurt, garlic, nutmeg and salt and pepper to taste. Serve in a small bowl or jug.

When the skins are cooked, remove from the oven and pile onto a large plate. Serve at once with a bowl of garlic sauce for dipping.

# ain courses & light meals

(Continued)

 **ain courses & light meals**

Braised soy cod

Serves 4

There's more to cod than just parsley sauce. Here's a cheerful Chinese-style dish which brings out the best of its many virtues.

Like all stir-fried dishes, it is important to have all the ingredients assembled beforehand and ready to go. This can be done in advance, leaving only the final cooking, which takes less than 10 minutes. Accompany with boiled brown rice and a crisp green salad.

Lynda Brown

2 tablespoons sun-
flower oil
4 spring onions, finely
chopped
1 dessertspoon fresh
root ginger, finely
chopped
1¼ lb (500 g) cod,
preferably from the
thick end, skinned,
boned and cut into
large cubes
½ red pepper, de-
seeded and cut into
thin strips
Shredded spring
onion, to garnish
Sauce
2 tablespoons dark soy
sauce
1 tablespoon sugar
1 tablespoon cornflour
2 tablespoons dry
sherry

For the sauce, mix the soy sauce and sugar with 4 tablespoons water and set aside. Mix the cornflour to a smooth paste with 1 tablespoon water and set aside.

Heat the oil in a wok or very large frying-pan over a high heat. Add the spring onions and ginger and stir-fry for a few seconds, then add the cod and red pepper. Reduce the heat slightly and cook for 3–4 minutes, gently turning the cod pieces over and around until they begin to brown, but taking care not to break them up too much.

Pour in the sherry, followed by the soy sauce mixture. Simmer very gently 4–5 minutes until the fish is just cooked through. Stir in the cornflour mixture and cook for a further 2 minutes to thicken the sauce and cook the cornflour. Transfer carefully to a serving dish and garnish with a shredded spring onion. Serve at once.

Cod braised with leeks in cider

Serves 4

Cooked by this method, the fish absorbs the flavour of the leek and enhances the cider during cooking to produce a lovely sauce. Oak vat cider is cider that has been aged in oak casks for one year. Some cider is blended but oak vat is sold straight from the cask. You'll find it labelled as 'traditional' and it has a cloudy appearance.

Kevin Woodford

1 tablespoon sunflower oil
2 oz (50 g) onion, finely diced
4 oz (100 g) leek, diced and well rinsed
1 lb (450 g) cod, skinned and cut into 2 in (5 cm) pieces
Salt and freshly ground black pepper
10 fl oz (300 ml) cider, oak vat cider if possible
Juice of ½ lemon
4 fl oz (120 ml) top of the milk
½ oz (12.5 g) butter

Heat the oil in a large frying-pan. Add the onion and leek and cook for 3–4 minutes. Add the fish pieces, season to taste with salt and pepper and cover with the cider. Bring to the boil, reduce the heat to a simmer, cover and cook 6–8 minutes until the fish is cooked through.

Remove the fish and vegetables from the liquid with a slotted spoon, cover with aluminium foil and keep warm. Bring the cooking liquid to the boil, add the lemon juice and milk and continue boiling until one third of the liquid has evaporated. Remove from the heat and whisk in the butter. Adjust the seasoning, if necessary. Pour the sauce over the fish, leeks and onion. Serve at once.

Cod cutlets en papillote

Serves 2

2 × 6 oz (175 g) cod
  cutlets
1 oz (25 g) butter, plus
  a little extra for the
  parcels
¹/₂ small lemon
Salt and freshly ground
  black pepper
Fresh parsley, to
  garnish

I love the aroma that fills the air as the parcels are opened up when I serve this dish.

Phil Diamond

Pre-heat the oven to gas mark 5, 375°F (190°C).

Butter 2 pieces of aluminium foil, each large enough to enclose a cod cutlet. Dot each cutlet with a little butter and add a squeeze of lemon juice and season to taste with salt and pepper. Fold over the foil edges to make a loose parcel completely enclosing the cutlets and put them on a baking tray. Cook for 20 minutes until the fish is cooked through and flakes easily. To serve, open parcels and garnish with parsley.

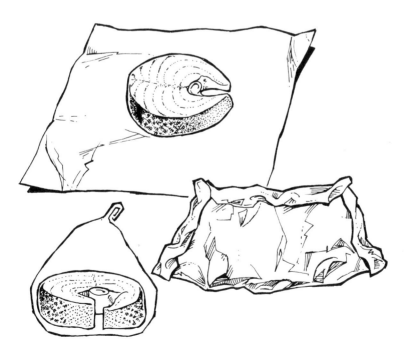

Florentine cod cutlets

Serves 4

Any other white fish cutlet is also suitable for this tasty dish.

Phil Diamond

1¹/₂ lb (750 g) fresh spinach, trimmed and rinsed
4 oz (100 g) hard cheese such as Cheddar, grated
2 fl oz (50 ml) single cream or top of the milk
4 × 6 oz (175 g) cod cutlets
1 oz (25 g) butter
Pinch of paprika

Cook the spinach in enough boiling water to cover for 4–5 minutes, then drain thoroughly and chop finely. Put the spinach in a large saucepan over a low heat. Add the cheese, stirring gently until it melts, then stir in the cream or milk.

Pre-heat the grill to high.

Dot the cod cutlets with butter and place on the grill rack, then cook for 5 minutes each side. Spread the spinach paste over one side of each cutlet, sprinkle a little paprika and return to the grill for 3 minutes until lightly browned. Serve at once.

Special kedgeree

Serves 4

Kedgeree is an inexpensive dish because the rice makes a little fish go a long way. If you want to make it more special and slightly richer, the beaten eggs that I have used do just that.

Phil Diamond

1 lb (450 g) smoked haddock fillets
2 oz (50 g) butter
4 oz (100 g) long-grain rice, cooked
3 tablespoons top of the milk
3 eggs, size 1, beaten
Salt and freshly ground black pepper
Chopped fresh parsley, to garnish
Toast triangles, to serve

Poach the haddock fillet in boiling water for 10 minutes. Lift out with a slotted spoon, remove the skin and flake the flesh.

Melt the butter in a large saucepan over a low heat, add the haddock and cooked rice and gently mix. Increase the heat and add the milk with the eggs, then stir gently until eggs set. Season to taste with salt and pepper and garnish with parsley. Serve with triangles of toast.

Grilled plaice with sweet paprika and garlic

Serves 2

Since my wife Maureen first tried this dish out on me many years ago, it has become a firm favourite with our friends and customers. Your fishmonger will be happy to prepare the fish for you.

Phil Diamond

1 oz (25 g) butter
2 × 12 oz–1 lb (350–450 g) whole plaice, cleaned, headed and trimmed
1 garlic clove, crushed
$1/2$ oz (15 g) ground sweet paprika
Salt and freshly ground pepper

Pre-heat the grill to high. Lightly grease the base of the grill pan with a little butter.

Slash both sides of the fish 2 or 3 times and place them in the grill pan, dark side up. Dot the fish with a little butter and sprinkle with garlic and paprika. Grill for 5 minutes, basting occasionally, then turn the fish over and grill a further 5 minutes or until the fish is cooked through and flakes easily. Carefully transfer the fish to a warmed serving dish and pour over juices from the grill pan. Season to taste with salt and pepper.

Fried herring in cornflakes

Serves 4

My son, Garry, loves herrings and he also loves cornflakes. One day we combined the two with great results!

Phil Diamond

4 large herrings, filleted
flour for dusting
2 eggs, beaten
4 oz (100 g) cornflakes, crushed
Sunflower oil for shallow frying
Chopped fresh parsley and lemon quarters, to garnish

Wash the herring fillets and pat dry with kitchen paper. Dust the fillets with flour, then dip them into the eggs and coat them with cornflakes on both sides.

Heat the oil in a frying-pan, and shallow fry the fillets for about 4 minutes each side. Drain the fish well on kitchen paper. Garnish with chopped parsley and lemon quarters and serve.

Steamed grey mullet

Serves 2

I was very surprised when I first tried this recipe at the wonderful flavour it gave the mullet. This fish is at its cheapest in the autumn and winter months.

Phil Diamond

2 × 12 oz (350 g) grey mullet, headed, cleaned and scaled
1 teaspoon salt
4 spring onions, thinly sliced lengthways
1 oz (25 g) butter
1 tablespoon dark soy sauce

Wash the mullets and pat dry with kitchen paper. Rub a little salt into the fish inside and out, then set aside.

Set up steamer; if you haven't got one you can use 2 large deep dinner plates over a saucepan of boiling water. Place most of the spring onions, butter and soy sauce inside the cavities of the fish, then dot the outsides with the remaining butter, soy sauce and spring onions.

Place the fish in the steamer and steam for 15 minutes or until cooked through and the fish flakes easily. Serve at once.

Steamed trout fillets

Serves 2

Now that trout are so successfully farmed they are far cheaper than they used to be. Serve these tender fillets with a steamed green vegetable and boiled potatoes.

Phil Diamond

2 × 12–14 oz (350–400 g) trout, filleted
Juice and finely grated zest of ¹/₄ lemon
¹/₂ oz (12.5 g) butter
Lemon twists and fresh parsley, to garnish

Bring a large saucepan of water to the boil.

Place the 4 trout fillets on an oven-proof dinner plate large enough to fit over the pan, sprinkle with the lemon zest and juice and dot with butter. Cover with a second dinner plate, then place on top of the saucepan and steam for 8 minutes or until cooked through and the flesh flakes easily. Garnish with lemon twists and parsley. Serve at once.

Soused grilled mackerel

Serves 4

4 large mackerel fillets
6 fl oz (175 ml) malt
  vinegar
¼ oz (10 g) mixed
  pickling spice
2 bay leaves
1 garlic clove, crushed

I have eaten all sorts of fried or grilled fish that have first been soused in this way – they taste absolutely wonderful.

Phil Diamond

Bring the vinegar and 4 fl oz (120 ml) water to the boil in a small saucepan, then add the pickling spice, bay leaves and garlic and continue boiling for 4 minutes. Take off heat and set aside.

Cover a grill rack with aluminium foil. Place the 4 fillets on the rack and grill under high heat for 3 minutes each side or until cooked through and the flesh flakes easily.

Carefully lift the fillets with a fish slice and place them in a deep serving dish, skin side up. Pour the marinade over the fillets, not quite covering them, then cover and refrigerate for at least 6 hours, gently turning once. Serve cold as a starter, or, in summer, as a main dish with a crisp salad.

Stuffed sprats

Serves 4

Sprats are in season from September to March and, like herring and mackerel, are ideal for grilling or baking as they are rich in natural oils. Serve this cheap and tasty dish with sweet red cabbage and boiled potatoes.

Phil Diamond

1¹/₂ lb (750 g) fresh sprats
4 oz (100 g) hard cheese such as Cheddar, grated
2 oz (50 g) dried white breadcrumbs
¹/₂ teaspoon dried oregano
1 tablespoon milk
2 eggs
2 oz (50 g) seasoned flour
Sunflower oil for frying (optional)

Prepare the sprats by cutting off the heads and tails, then splitting each fish the full length of the belly and remove the guts. Open each fish on its belly and press down firmly along the back with your thumb, loosening the bones – the spine will then easily pull away from the flesh, leaving you with a butterfly fillet. Prepare all the sprats in the same manner. Wash each fish and pat dry with kitchen paper, then set aside.

Mix the cheese, breadcrumbs, oregano, milk and 1 egg together. Make a sandwich of two butterfly fillets with a little stuffing, then coat the fish parcels with the seasoned flour on both sides and dip them in the other beaten egg. Set aside.

To shallow fry
Heat a thin layer of sunflower oil in a frying-pan and add the sprats in a single layer; cook in several batches if necessary. Fry for about 2 minutes, then gently turn over and fry on the other side for a further 2 minutes until golden brown and cooked through. Drain well on kitchen paper.

To bake
Pre-heat the oven to gas mark 4, 350°F (180°C). Place the sprats in a single

layer in an ovenproof dish and cook for 15–20 minutes or until cooked through.

To grill
Pre-heat the grill to high. Place the sprats on the grill rack and grill for 5 minutes on each side until golden brown and cooked through.

Huss kebabs

Serves 4

Hot boiled rice and an onion and tomato salad are the ideal accompaniments for these flavoursome kebabs. If you can afford the prawns, they add an extra sparkle.

Phil Diamond

1 lb (450 g) skinned huss fillets, cut into 1 in (2.5 cm) cubes
1 large green pepper, de-seeded and cut into 1 in squares
1 large red pepper, de-seeded and cut into 1 in squares
4 oz (100 g) prawns in shells (optional)
4 oz (100 g) button mushrooms
Marinade
2 tablespoons sun-flower oil
1 tablespoon light soy sauce
1 tablespoon white wine vinegar
Salt and freshly ground black pepper

Alternately thread the huss, peppers, prawns (if using) and mushrooms onto 8 small or 4 large skewers.

Mix together the oil, soy sauce, white wine vinegar and salt and pepper to taste. Brush the marinade over the kebabs and set aside for 15 minutes.

Pre-heat the grill to medium high. Place the kebabs on the grill rack and grill for 15 minutes, turning and basting frequently. Serve at once.

Seafood bread and butter pudding

Serves 1

A savoury bread and butter pudding may sound like an odd idea, but don't be put off. It's actually a very quick and delicious way of turning an ordinary sandwich into a special lunch dish. And if you make it when the oven is already being used for baking, you won't even be spending out on fuel. You don't have to use prawns and tomato in your sandwich – try cheese and tomato, with a hint of mustard, or cheese and ham, perhaps. One thing I would avoid, though, is cheese and pickle, which might end up as a rather unpleasant mess!

Sophie Grigson

Butter
2 large slices whole-meal or granary bread
¹⁄₂ tomato, seeded and diced
1 oz (25 g) cooked and peeled prawns
A squeeze of lemon juice
A few leaves of fresh tarragon, chopped
Salt and freshly ground black pepper
5 fl oz (150 ml) milk
1 egg

Pre-heat the oven to gas mark 4, 350°F (180°C).

Butter the slices of bread and cut off the crusts. Mix the tomato with the prawns, lemon juice, tarragon and salt and pepper to taste. Make a thick sandwich with this mixture, then cut into quarters. Pack the quarters tightly into a small, lightly buttered ovenproof dish.

Beat the milk with the egg and salt and pepper to taste, then pour over the sandwich. Cook for 30 minutes until the custard is just set, and the upper layer of bread is lightly browned.

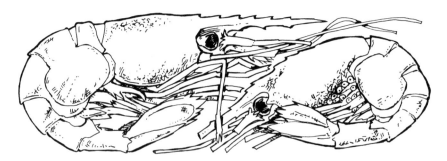

Phil's mussels

Serves 4

Mussels are in season from September through till April and this is a recipe where you could put leftover Christmas cheer (the vermouth) to good use! Serve with chunks of crusty French bread to soak wonderful liquor.

Phil Diamond

4 lb (1.75 kg) mussels (about 4 pints)
2 oz (50 g) butter
2 tablespoons sunflower oil
1 large onion, sliced into rings
4 oz (100 g) tomato purée
14 fl oz (400 ml) sweet vermouth
4 garlic cloves, crushed
1/2–1 large red pepper, de-seeded and thinly sliced
1/2–1 large green pepper, de-seeded and thinly sliced
1/2–1 large yellow pepper, de-seeded and thinly sliced
Finely chopped fresh parsley, to garnish

Discard all broken mussels and any mussels that won't close after giving them a sharp tap. De-beard, scrape and wash the remainder, then set aside. Melt the butter in a large saucepan with a lid. Add the oil, then sauté the onions and add the tomato purée, 14 fl oz (400 ml) water and vermouth and bring to the boil. Add the garlic and peppers. After 5 minutes lower the heat, cover, and simmer for 10 minutes. Turn the heat up to medium and add all the mussels. Cover and cook for 7 minutes. Uncover and stir, then bring the bottom mussels to the top. Do this continuously until all the mussels open, discarding any that remain closed. This should take about 10 minutes. Take the saucepan off the heat and spoon the mussels into 4 serving bowls. Bring the liquid left in the pan to the boil, then pour over the mussels and sprinkle over the parsley.

Chicken and orange hot-pot with herby scones

Chicken and orange is really a delicious combination. The warm herby scones, which accompany the dish, make this hot-pot a very substantial meal.

Lesley Waters

Serves 4

1 tablespoon vegetable oil
1 oz (25 g) butter
3¹/₂ lb (1.5 kg) chicken, jointed into 8 pieces
1 large onion, sliced
1 oz (25 g) plain flour
Grated zest of 2 oranges
10 fl oz (300 ml) orange juice
1 bay leaf
10 fl oz (300 ml) chicken or vegetable stock
1 garlic clove, crushed
4 oz (100 g) split lentils, rinsed and picked over
5 fl oz (150 ml) single cream
Chopped fresh parsley, to garnish
Scones
8 oz (225 g) self-raising flour
½ teaspoon salt
1 oz (25 g) margarine
1 teaspoon dried mixed herbs
2 oz (50 g) Cheddar cheese, grated
5 fl oz (150 ml) milk

Pre-heat the oven to gas mark 8, 450°F (230°C).

To make the scones, sift the flour and the salt into a bowl. Add the margarine and rub in with fingertips. Then add the herbs and cheese and mix to a soft dough with the milk. Turn out onto a lightly floured surface and quickly knead.

Roll out to ½ in (1 cm) thick and cut into scones. Place them on a greased baking tray and brush the tops with a little milk or sprinkle with flour. Bake for 8–10 minutes. Cool on a wire rack.

Lower the oven temperature to gas mark 4, 350°F (180°C).

Melt the oil and butter in a large, deep frying-pan, add the chicken pieces and brown on all sides. Remove from the pan and, if desired, skin the chicken. Place in an ovenproof casserole. Add the onion to the frying-pan and cook until lightly browned. Add the flour and cook for 30 seconds, then add the orange zest and juice, bay leaf, stock, garlic and lentils. Bring to the boil and pour into the casserole.

Cover and bake for 1¹/₂ hours, basting occasionally, until the chicken is tender and cooked through.

Skim off any excess fat from the surface, then stir in the single cream. Sprinkle with parsley and serve.

Chicken and aubergine lasagne

Serves 6

Lasagne is a time-consuming dish to put together. But if you make the sauces rather more liquid than you would normally, you don't have to pre-cook the dried sheets of pasta.

Sophie Grigson

3 tablespoons sun-
flower or olive oil
3 chicken breasts,
skinned and cut into
¹/₂ in (1 cm) cubes
1 onion, chopped
2 garlic cloves,
chopped
1 small aubergine, cut
into ¹/₂ in (1 cm)
cubes
1¹/₂ × 14 oz (397 g) can
tomatoes, or 1¹/₂ lb
(750 g) fresh tom-
atoes, skinned and
coarsely chopped
1¹/₂ tablespoons
chopped fresh basil,
or 1 teaspoon dried
oregano
1¹/₂ teaspoons sugar
1 teaspoon red wine
vinegar
1 tablespoon tomato
paste
Salt and freshly ground
black pepper
6 oz (175 g) dried green
or white lasagne
2 oz (50 g) Parmesan
cheese, freshly
grated
(cont. overleaf)

Heat 1 tablespoon oil in a large frying-pan, then add the chicken and cook until sealed on all sides. Remove from the pan, then add the onion and garlic and fry until softened but not coloured. Add the remaining oil and the aubergine and sauté for a further 5 minutes. Return the chicken to the pan with the tomatoes, herbs, sugar, vinegar, tomato paste and salt and pepper to taste. If you use canned tomatoes, break them up with the edge of the spoon. Bring to the boil, reduce to a simmer and cook for 5 minutes until the aubergine is soft. The sauce should still be fairly liquid.

To make the Béchamel sauce, melt the butter in a medium-sized pan, then stir in the flour. Cook for 1 minute, remove from the heat and gradually stir in the milk. Return to the heat, season to taste with salt and pepper, and simmer gently for 10 minutes.

Pre-heat the oven to gas mark 5, 375°F (190°C).

Brush a 10 × 10 in (25 × 25 cm) ovenproof dish, or a 12 in (30 cm) long oval gratin dish, with olive oil. Spread a thin layer of Béchamel on the base. Cover with a layer of lasagne, leaving a small gap between each sheet and taking care not to overlap. Use broken up pieces to fill

43

Béchamel sauce
1 oz (25 g) butter
1 oz (25 g) plain flour
1 pt (600 ml) milk

the spaces. Spoon over half of the chicken and aubergine mixture, spreading to cover the lasagne. Then spoon one third of the remaining Béchamel over this. Sprinkle with a little Parmesan cheese. Repeat these layers, then add a final layer of lasagne, cover completely with Béchamel and sprinkle with the remaining Parmesan.

Cover with aluminium foil and cook for 20 minutes. Remove the foil and continue cooking for a further 25–30 minutes. Uncover and let it sit for 5 minutes before serving.

Chicken joints in pastry

Serves 4

Pushing cottage cheese flavoured with fresh herbs between the skin and flesh of these chicken joints helps to keep the flesh moist while they cook. If you are unable to get hold of the herbs suggested, substitute other fresh ones rather than dried, or increase the quantity of parsley. Serve with melted butter or plain yoghurt, flavoured with extra chopped herbs.

Sophie Grigson

8 oz (225 g) cottage
cheese
1 tablespoon *each*
chopped fresh
parsley, chives and
mint or basil
1–2 tablespoons lemon
juice
Salt and cayenne
pepper
4 chicken joints
12 oz (350 g) puff pastry,
thawed if frozen
1 egg, beaten

Pre-heat the oven to gas mark 8, 450°F (230°C).

Drain the cottage cheese well, then push through a sieve with a wooden spoon. Mix with the herbs, lemon juice, salt and cayenne pepper to taste. Push your fingers carefully under the skin of the chicken joints, easing the skin away from the flesh without detaching it completely. Using a teaspoon, stuff the cottage cheese mixture into the gap, smoothing it down so each joint is evenly filled.

Divide the pastry into 4 equal pieces and roll out each piece on a lightly floured surface so it is large enough to wrap up 1 of the chicken joints. Brush the edges with water to seal, then wrap each joint in the pastry, pressing the edges together and tucking all joins underneath. Trim any excess pastry and use to make flowers or leaves for decoration. Place the parcels on a baking tray and brush with the egg.

Cook for 15 minutes or until pastry begins to brown, then lower the heat to gas mark 5, 375°F (190°C) and cook for a further 15 minutes. Test one parcel for 'doneness' as discreetly as you can with a skewer; the chicken is cooked through when all the juice runs clear. Serve at once.

Chicken collops in mustard and mushroom sauce

Serves 4

The term 'collops', also known as esca-lopes, means $1/2$ in (1 cm) thick slices taken from across the chicken breast. This recipe produces a dish of moist chicken pieces in a creamy sauce. If you buy chicken breast portions on the bone and bone and skin each one yourself (see illustrations) you can make stock from the trimmings in which to cook rice to accompany this dish.

Kevin Woodford

4 chicken supremes (boneless and skinned chicken breasts available in most supermarkets or butchers), or 4 breast joints, boned and skinned
2 oz (50 g) butter
Salt and freshly ground black pepper

Cut the breasts into collops. Melt the butter in a large frying-pan, then add the chicken pieces, season to taste with salt and pepper and quickly cook on both sides. Remove from the pan; set aside and keep warm.

Add the onion, mushrooms, garlic, parsley and tarragon to the pan and cook for 2–3 minutes, then add the cream, or milk, and mustard. Bring to the boil and season with salt and pepper. Reduce the heat to a simmer,

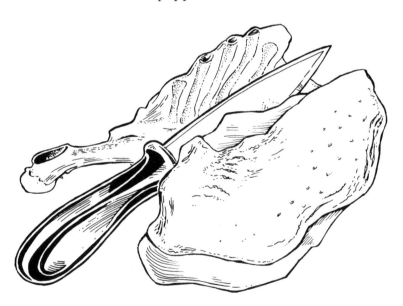

2 oz (50 g) onion, finely
    chopped
2 oz (50 g) mushrooms,
    sliced
1 garlic clove, crushed
½ teaspoon chopped
    fresh parsley
1 teaspoon chopped
    fresh tarragon
4 fl oz (120 ml) single
    cream or top of the
    milk
¼ tablespoon French
    mustard

return the chicken pieces to the pan
and simmer for 4 minutes. Serve on a
hot plate with the rice or vegetables of
your choice.

Carol's meaty stew

Serves 4

*This is a warming winter dish to which
you could also add suet dumplings or a
'cobbler' (scone) topping.*

Carol Smith, Wearside

1 tablespoon sunflower
    oil
¾ lb (350 g) shin beef,
    fat removed and cut
    into small pieces
1 large onion, sliced
1 small turnip, diced
2 large potatoes, diced
1 stick celery, chopped
1 dessertspoon tomato
    purée
1 tablespoon flour
10 fl oz (300 ml) stock,
    heated
3 oz (75 g) haricot
    beans, soaked
Salt and freshly ground
    black pepper

Heat the oil in a pan and fry the meat
and vegetables until lightly browned.
Stir in the tomato purée and the flour
and gradually add the hot stock. Add
the soaked beans. Bring to the boil,
season and transfer to a covered casserole dish. Cook in the oven for 2
hours at gas mark 3, 325°F (160°C).
Alternatively, this is an ideal dish for
a slow cooker. Cook on LOW for 7–8
hours.

Beefy ale bake

Serves 4

This inexpensive casserole smells wonder-ful while it's cooking and it tastes even better.

Bazaar Viewer

1¹/₂ lb (750 g) stewing beef
2 tablespoons sun-flower oil
1 large onion, thinly sliced
8 oz (225 g) carrots, peeled and sliced
1¹/₂ oz (40 g) flour
15 fl oz (450 ml) brown ale
6 oz (175 g) mushrooms, sliced
1 teaspoon tomato purée
Bay leaf
Salt and pepper
1 × 5 oz (150 g) tub natural yoghurt
Topping
3 oz (75 g) English cheese, grated
1 oz (25 g) sunflower margarine
1 small French loaf
Made mustard

Cut the beef into cubes, discarding any skin or fat. Heat the oil in a large saucepan, add the beef and cook until browned on all sides.
Remove from the pan and put to one side. Add the onion and carrot and fry until they start to change colour. Stir in the flour and cook until caramel brown. Remove the pan from the heat and gradually stir in the ale. Return to the heat and bring to the boil, stirring all the time. Add the mushrooms, tomato purée, bay leaf, seasonings and meat. Pour into a casserole dish, cover and bake in the oven on gas mark 3, 325°F (160°C) for 1¹/₂ hours. Stir in the yoghurt.
To prepare the topping, mash to-gether the cheese and margarine. Cut the French bread into 8 slices, spread a little mustard over each, then the cheese mixture. Place the bread slices, cheese side upwards, on top of the meat. Raise the oven temperature to gas mark 5, 375°F (190°C) and bake, uncovered, until the topping is crisp and golden.

Ginger and honey lamb kebabs

Serves 2

This sticky, aromatic marinade can also be used to marinate chicken pieces or spare-ribs. It can be made in advance and kept in the fridge for up to one week. Meat mari-nated this way is particularly good when barbecued.

Sophie Grigson

12 oz (350 g) lean bone-less lamb, cubed
12 pearl onions
1 red pepper, de-seeded and cut in 1 in (2.5 cm) cubes
Marinade
1 in (2.5 cm) piece fresh root ginger, peeled and finely chopped
1 garlic clove, finely chopped
3 tablespoons sun-flower oil and 3 of sesame oil, or all sunflower oil
2 tablespoons clear honey
1 tablespoon dark soy sauce
Juice of ½ lemon

To make the marinade, place the gin-ger and garlic in a pan with the oil, honey, soy sauce and lemon juice. Heat very gently, stirring, until the honey is completely dissolved, then set aside to cool.

Place the lamb in a glass bowl and pour in the marinade, turning the meat to coat well. Cover and leave in the fridge for 1–2 hours, turning and basting meat occasionally.

Meanwhile, pour boiling water over the onions and leave for 30 seconds. Drain and skin, then simmer in lightly salted water until half cooked. Drain well and set aside. Pre-heat the grill to high.

Make up the kebabs, alternating cubes of lamb, pepper and onions, and brush with the marinade. Grill the kebabs, turning frequently and basting with marinade, until the lamb is just cooked but still slightly pink in the centre.

Lamb and cracked wheat pilaf

Serves 4

Cracked wheat, or bulgar, is a grain I use often. It can be bought from health food shops and most supermarkets and is a popular staple in the Middle East. It's made by lightly crushing wheat grains which are partially cooked, giving it a mild, nutty flavour. Because of this, it needs only to be soaked or cooked in water for a very short time. It also swells up considerably, so again you need very little, 2–3 oz (50–75 g) per person. Because cracked wheat is so easy to use, this is one of my favourite grains. Use it wherever you would use rice – in pilafs, salads or stuffings.

This is a basic recipe which can be adapted any way you please. Non-meat variations, with quartered hard-boiled eggs on top and some toasted flaked almonds scattered over, are equally delicious.

Lynda Brown

1 tablespoon sunflower oil for frying
1 small onion, finely chopped
1 fresh green chilli, seeds removed and finely chopped (optional)
6 oz (175 g) lean minced lamb
1 teaspoon ground cinnamon, allspice or mixed spice
8–10 oz (225–275 g) cracked wheat
1 tablespoon tomato purée
2 oz (50 g) dried dates, coarsely chopped or halved

Measure water, allowing twice the amount of water to cracked wheat – either 16 or 20 fl oz (475 or 600 ml) – and set aside.

Heat the oil in a large frying-pan. Add the onion and chilli if using and cook until softened. Add the lamb, stir about to break it up and continue cooking until nicely browned. Sprinkle in the spice and stir in the cracked wheat. Add the tomato purée and water.

Bring to the boil, scatter in the raisins and dates, reduce the heat to a simmer, cover and gently cook for 4–5 minutes. Turn off the heat to let the wheat soften completely and the flavours develop; it will continue to cook in its own steam.

Meanwhile, heat the extra oil or

2 tablespoons raisins or sultanas
A little extra sunflower oil or butter
4–6 oz (100–175 g) carrots, cut into thin strips
8 oz (225 g) hot cooked peas

butter in a small pan. Add the carrots and cook until soft and well browned at the edges, turning often.

To serve, pile the pilaf lightly into a serving dish. Put the carrots down the centre and surround with the cooked peas. If you like, stir a few peas into the pilaf first.

Chinese spare ribs

Serves 4

This exotic marinade turns spare ribs into an oriental feast. Serve them with rice and salad or stir-fried vegetables.

Margaret Loh, Malvern

1 tablespoon sunflower oil
2 tablespoons clear honey or golden syrup
1 tablespoon dark soy sauce
1 tablespoon dry sherry
1/2 teaspoon 5-spice powder (available from oriental grocers) or mixed spice
1/2 teaspoon salt
2 tablespoons orange juice
1 1/2–1 3/4 lb (750 g) pork spare ribs

Mix all the marinade ingredients together, and coat the spare ribs well. Leave in a shallow glass or china dish to marinate for 30 minutes, turning once or twice. Pre-heat the grill and grill the ribs for 10 minutes or so until well done. Alternatively you can bake them at gas mark 8, 450°F (230°C) for about 30 minutes.

Jambalaya

Serves 4

When you only have a little ham left and don't know what to do with it, this is a really good dish to make. Sweet peppers are expensive but I grow my own on a sunny windowsill using the seeds from a bought green pepper. Surplus peppers are de-seeded, sliced, diced and frozen, ready for a dish such as this.

Shirley Goode

4 oz (100 g) bacon rashers, diced
1 onion, finely chopped
1 green pepper, de-seeded and cut into strips
8 oz (250 g) long-grain rice
1 × 14 oz (397 g) can tomatoes, drained and chopped
8 oz (225 g) ham, diced
1 teaspoon dried thyme
Salt and freshly ground black pepper
15 fl oz (450 ml) chicken stock
A few peeled cooked prawns (optional)
2 small bananas, peeled and sliced
Finely chopped fresh parsley, to garnish

Fry the bacon in a large, heavy frying-pan until brown but not crisp. Drain well on kitchen paper and set aside. Add the onion to the bacon fat and cook slowly for 2 minutes. Stir in the green pepper and rice, stirring until the rice turns transparent. Add the tomatoes, bacon, ham, thyme and salt and pepper to taste.

Pour in 10 fl oz (300 ml) chicken stock, cover and simmer for 10 minutes. Add the prawns if using. Heat the remaining stock and add a little at a time, stirring, until it becomes absorbed and the rice is tender. Stir in the bananas. Serve on a warmed dish, garnished with the parsley.

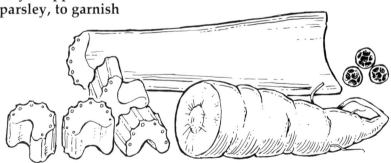

Braised oxtail

Serves 4

Of all the dishes based upon slow-cooked meat this is my favourite. Oxtail is very meaty and gives its cooking liquid the most superb flavour and aroma. This is a dish which demands to be picked up and eaten using the fingers, and I recall many happy meals drawing the last drops of flavour from the bone. It is always a good idea to serve it with a small bowl of warm water and a serviette so you and your guests can clean up after the meal! I usually keep back a little of the sauce for the following day and serve myself a large bowl of oxtail soup just by re-heating it.

Kevin Woodford

1 fl oz (25 ml) sunflower oil
2½ lb (1.25 kg) oxtail, chopped
4 oz (100 g) carrots, chopped
4 oz (100 g) onions, chopped
4 oz (100 g) leeks, sliced and well rinsed
4 oz (100 g) celery, chopped
2 oz (50 g) plain flour
2 oz (50 g) tomato purée
2¼ pints (1.25 litres) hot beef stock
Salt and freshly ground black pepper
Bouquet garni
Selection of freshly boiled vegetables, to serve

Pre-heat the oven to gas mark 6, 400°F (200°C).

Heat the oil in a large, heavy based saucepan, then add the oxtail and cook to seal on both sides. Remove from the pan with a slotted spoon. Add the chopped vegetables to the hot oil and cook for 5–6 minutes, stirring constantly. Add the flour and mix thoroughly into the oil and vegetables, ensuring all of the oil has been absorbed into the flour. Continue cooking for 3–4 minutes, then mix in the tomato purée. Gradually stir in the stock, stirring constantly, then return the oxtail to the sauce. Season to taste with salt and pepper, add the bouquet garni and cover tightly.

Cook for 2½–3 hours. To serve, simply transfer the meat, vegetables and sauce into a warm serving dish and add some freshly boiled vegetables of your choice, to put some lovely fresh colour into the dish.

Grilled lambs' kidneys with herb butter

Serves 4 as a first course,
2 as a main course

Don't spoil delicate little lambs' kidneys by overcooking them – they become tough, dull in flavour and a total waste of money. At their best they should still be slightly pink in the centre, tender and mild.

Sophie Grigson

8 lambs' kidneys
1 bunch fresh
watercress
Sunflower oil
Salt and freshly ground
black pepper
Herb butter
2 oz (50 g) butter,
softened
1 generous tablespoon
chopped fresh herbs,
such as parsley,

To make the herb butter, beat the butter with the herbs, lemon juice and cayenne pepper until well mixed. Form into a cylinder on a sheet of greaseproof paper, wrap and chill, or pile into a small bowl, cover and chill.

If necessary, remove the outer membrane of the kidneys. Split in half, from the outer curved edge to the inner curved edge without cutting right through. Open each kidney out to form a rosette, and snip out the

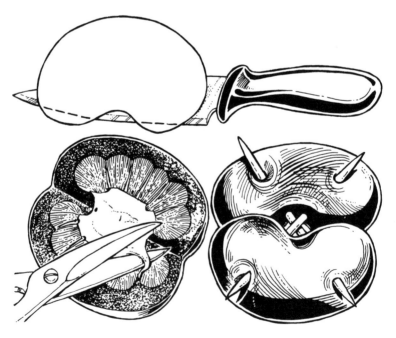

chives, marjoram,
tarragon or mint
1–2 tablespoons lemon
juice
Cayenne pepper

tough inner core with a small pair of scissors or a knife. To keep each kidney flat as it cooks, secure with 2 wooden cocktail sticks, threaded through the rosette at right angles to form a cross.

Pre-heat the grill to high. Wash and pick over the watercress. Dry with kitchen paper and arrange on a serving dish. Brush the kidneys with oil and season lightly. Cook under the hot grill for 6 minutes, turning once. Remove the sticks, and lay the kidneys on the bed of watercress, topping each kidney with a slice of herb butter. Serve quickly while the kidneys are still piping hot, serving any remaining butter separately.

Liver Portuguese-style

Serves 2

This quick dish should be served on a bed of rice. I like to add a chicken stock cube or a pinch of turmeric to the water I cook the rice in to give it extra flavour.

Lynda Rowley, Crewkerne

4 oz (100 g) lamb's liver
2 oz (50 g) wholemeal
flour, seasoned
2 tablespoons sun-
flower oil
½ onion, chopped
5 fl oz (150 ml) red
wine or stock
1 teaspoon marjoram
2 tablespoons natural
yoghurt

Cut the liver into thin strips and dip in the seasoned flour. Heat the oil in a frying-pan and fry the liver until sealed on all sides. Add the chopped onion, reduce the heat and cook until the onion is transparent. Stir in the red wine and marjoram and cook for a few minutes over a high heat to concentrate the liquid. Take off the heat and stir in the yoghurt. Serve immediately.

Haggis

Serves 4

*Too good a dish to keep just for Burns'
night (25th January) or St Andrew's night
(30th November) when the Scots traditionally serve it, Haggis is a filling and
economical supper to enjoy all year round.
Steam it in a pudding basin and serve
with equal quantities of creamy mashed
potatoes and mashed swedes mixed with
plenty of ground black pepper and butter.*

Gill MacLennan

**4 oz (100 g) lamb's
heart
4 oz (100 g) lamb's
liver, skinned
4 oz (100 g) lean bone-
less lamb
4 oz (100 g) shredded
suet
4 oz (100 g) pinhead
oatmeal, toasted
until golden
1 small onion, chopped
1 teaspoon ground
black pepper
1 teaspoon dried mixed
herbs
1 teaspoon salt
1 teaspoon ground
allspice
1/2 teaspoon cayenne
pepper
1/2 teaspoon grated
nutmeg
10 fl oz (300 ml) beef or
lamb stock
Butter for greasing**

Cut out the tubes from the heart with
scissors. Finely chop the heart, liver
and lamb meat with a sharp knife,
process in a food processor or put
through a mincer. Place in a bowl
with the suet, oatmeal, onion,
pepper, herbs, salt, allspice, cayenne,
nutmeg and stock and stir well to mix.

Lightly butter a 1 lb (450 g) pudding
basin and spoon the mixture in. Cover
with greaseproof paper and foil and
place in a pan half-filled with boiling
water. Bring to the boil, reduce heat
to a simmering, cover and cook for 2
hours, topping up with boiling water
when necessary to prevent the pan
boiling dry. Serve piping hot.

Potato gnocchi

Serves 4

Gnocchi means 'little dumplings' in Italian. The best way to serve gnocchi is with a light tomato sauce (page 83) or, as in this recipe, simply by adding some butter, cheese and tomatoes to the drained gnocchi and finishing under the grill.

Gnocchi can be prepared in advance but only cook them just before you are ready to serve. Never re-heat them after being cooked.

Lesley Waters

1 lb (450 g) mashed
  potatoes
4 oz (100 g) plain flour
1 egg
1 egg yolk
2 oz (50 g) butter or
  sunflower margarine
Salt and freshly ground
  black pepper
Grated nutmeg
4 oz (100 g) Cheddar or
  blue cheese, grated
2 tomatoes, diced

Mix the mashed potato with the flour, egg, egg yolk, half the butter or margarine, and salt, pepper and nutmeg to taste. Dust your hands with flour and roll the potato mixture into a thick sausage on a lightly floured surface. Cut the roll into ³/₄ in (2 cm) lengths. Using floured hands, mould into balls, dust well with flour and flatten slightly with a fork.

To poach the gnocchi, place them in a large saucepan of boiling water. Cook until the gnocchi float to the surface, then continue cooking for a further 30 seconds. Drain carefully.

Pre-heat the grill. Place the gnocchi in a buttered flameproof serving dish. Sprinkle over the tomato and cheese and dot with the remaining butter or margarine. Grill until the gnocchi are slightly golden and bubbling. Serve at once.

Cabbage pie

Serves 4

A problem with British vegetable cookery is that it has never served cabbage well – look in your cookery books and you'll be hard put to find a decent recipe. Thankfully, other countries look more favourably on this ancient and noble vegetable. This recipe is based on the Russian dish kulebiaka.

It is a very adaptable dish. Here is a vegetarian version, but you can just as easily incorporate left-over chicken or bacon, or even a couple of good-quality cooked sausages. Some diced cooked potato is another good addition, as are herbs such as parsley and dill.

Never cook cabbage for more than 5 minutes, if you are serving it as a vegetable dish. After this time, the substances which give it its rank smell are released in far greater amounts, spoiling what can be a very fine and tasty vegetable. An egg wash brushed over the pie before it goes into the oven will give it a lovely golden brown shine. I like jacket potatoes with this dish. Choose medium-sized ones, cut them in half, paint the surfaces with oil, and they should be cooked by the time the pie is ready.

Lynda Brown

8 oz (225 g) cabbage, chopped
A little sunflower oil for frying
1 small onion, finely chopped
3–4 oz (75–100 g) mushrooms, wiped and chopped
2 hard-boiled eggs, chopped

Cook the cabbage in boiling water for 3–4 minutes. Drain well, pressing out all the excess moisture, then set aside. Heat the oil in a frying-pan. Add the onion and cook until softened, then add the mushrooms and continue cooking for a further 4–5 minutes. Mix with the cabbage, hard-boiled eggs, rice and any herbs you may want to use.

2 oz (50 g) brown or
   white cooked rice,
   slightly underdone
1–2 tablespoons
   chopped fresh herbs,
   or 1 teaspoon
   caraway seeds
   (optional)
12 oz (350 g) puff
   pastry, thawed if
   frozen

Pre-heat the oven to gas mark 6,
400°F (200°C).

Roll out the pastry on a lightly
floured surface to a large, thin rec-
tangle about 2 feet (60 cm) long. Pile
the cabbage in the centre, leaving
enough of the pastry at both ends to
fold over and enclose the filling. Bring
over the two ends and seal along the
edges, damping them first with water.
You should now have a pillow-shaped
parcel enclosing the filling. Decorate
with pastry trimmings, cut three
slashes across the centre and ease
gently onto a greased and floured
baking sheet.

Cook for 35–40 minutes until the
pastry is crisp and brown. If the top
looks like browning too quickly, turn
the heat down a little or move to a
lower shelf. Cool slightly before
serving.

Vegetable couscous

Serves 4

I first tasted couscous – a kind of hard wheat semolina – on holiday in North Africa, and couldn't wait to get home to cook it myself. This vegetarian version is not only an economical but a very tasty dish making the most of small amounts of a variety of vegetables.

Chickpeas are a traditional ingredient in couscous and add valuable protein. It is far cheaper to cook a whole pack of dried chickpeas (which can then be frozen, ready to use) than to buy them ready-cooked in cans.

Any of these vegetables are suitable for couscous: carrots, onions, turnips, swedes, parsnips, potatoes, courgettes, pumpkins, white cabbage, sweet peppers.

Shirley Goode

1 teaspoon dried chilli powder
2 teaspoons paprika
2 tablespoons sunflower oil
3 lb (1.5 kg) mixed vegetables (see above), chopped in equal-sized pieces
2 tablespoons tomato purée
1 lb (450 g) couscous
8 oz (225 g) cooked chickpeas

Sprinkle the chilli powder and paprika over the vegetables. Then heat the oil in a large saucepan and add the mixed vegetables. Stir well to coat all of them and fry for 2 minutes. Stir in the tomato purée and 1¼ pints (750 ml) water. Bring to the boil, reduce the heat and simmer, stirring occasionally.

Put the couscous in a large bowl and pour over 1 pint (600 ml) cold water. Stir well and leave to stand for 10 minutes. Add 1 pint (600 ml) boiling water and leave for a further 10 minutes. Strain the couscous into a steamer, pressing down to extract the excess water. Stir the chickpeas into the vegetables. Then place the steamer over the mixture and continue cooking until the vegetables are tender and the couscous is very hot.

Turn the couscous onto a warmed serving dish. Drain the vegetables and pour some of the juices over the couscous to moisten. Top with the vegetables. Serve the surplus juices in a gravy boat to add at table.

Black-eyed bean casserole

Serves 2

Although it is more expensive to buy cooked beans in cans, it does mean you can make meatless meals that much more speedily. All this casserole needs is a hunk of wholemeal bread to make a filling main course.

Gill MacLennan

1 tablespoon sunflower oil
1 large onion, chopped
1 garlic clove, chopped
1 oz (25 g) split red lentils, well rinsed and picked over
1 × 14 oz (397 g) can chopped tomatoes
1 × 14.6 oz (415 g) can black-eyed beans, or cooked yourself if you prefer
2 tablespoons crunchy peanut butter
¹/₂ teaspoon salt
Freshly ground black pepper

Heat the oil in a saucepan, add the onion and the garlic and fry for 7–10 minutes until golden brown.

Stir in the lentils, tomatoes with their juice, black-eyed beans and the liquid from the can, the peanut butter and salt and pepper to taste. Bring to the boil, reduce heat to a simmer, cover and cook for 20 minutes, stirring occasionally. Serve piping hot.

Leek and potato pie

Serves 4

The simplicity of this dish, coupled with its economy, matches the pleasure derived from the delightful flavour of the leeks and bacon. It makes an ideal snack, or is perfect for the busy cook who simply cannot afford the time to 'play' for too long in the kitchen and yet enjoys a tasty filling meal.

Kevin Woodford

2 lb (1 kg) potatoes, peeled, washed and diced
1 egg
1 oz (25 g) butter or sunflower margarine
Pinch of grated nutmeg
1 tablespoon sunflower oil
1¹/₂ lb (750 g) leeks, sliced and well rinsed
8 oz (225 g) streaky bacon rashers, rinded and chopped
Salt and freshly ground black pepper
Sauce
1¹/₂ oz (40 g) butter
1¹/₂ oz (40 g) plain flour
10 fl oz (300 ml) hot milk
3 oz (75 g) red Leicester cheese, grated

Pre-heat the oven to gas mark 3, 325°F (160°C).

Place the potatoes in a large saucepan with water to cover. Bring to the boil, then reduce heat to a simmer, cover and cook until tender. Drain well, then mash and beat in the egg, butter or margarine and nutmeg. Set aside to cool.

Heat the oil in a large frying-pan. Add the leeks and bacon and season to taste with salt and pepper. Cook for 3–4 minutes, stirring occasionally. Transfer to an ovenproof dish and set aside to cool.

To make the sauce, melt the butter in a heavy based saucepan. Add the flour, mix in well and cook for 2–3 minutes over a low heat. Gradually add the hot milk, stirring constantly, then add 2 oz (50 g) of the cheese and season to taste with salt and pepper.

Pour the sauce over the leek and bacon mixture and mix in well. Spread the potatoes over the top, fluff up with a fork and sprinkle with the remaining cheese. Cook for 15–20 minutes until golden brown. Serve at once.

Fresh noodles niçoise

Serves 4 (double the recipe if you are hungry – it's cheap enough!)

The difference between freshly produced pasta and the commercially made dried variety is enormous. For very little effort, time and money you can enjoy a plate full of delicious pasta.

Kevin Woodford

8 oz (225 g) plain flour
Salt and freshly ground black pepper
1 egg
4 egg yolks
2 teaspoons olive or sunflower oil
2 oz (50 g) butter
2 oz (50 g) onion, chopped
1 garlic clove, crushed
8 oz (225 g) fresh or tinned tomatoes, chopped
1 teaspoon chopped fresh parsley
¹/₂ oz (15 g) Parmesan or Cheddar cheese, finely grated

Sieve the flour and salt into a large bowl. Make a well in the centre and add the egg, yolks and oil. Mix to a smooth dough, cover with a damp cloth to prevent a skin forming and set aside for 10 minutes.

Roll out the dough on a lightly floured surface until thin, then cut into 2 pieces, each 3 × 12 in (7.5 × 30 cm). Set aside for 3 hours in a cool place.

Cut the dough into ⅛ in (3 mm) wide strips. Cook in a large saucepan of lightly salted boiling water for 12–15 minutes until *al dente*, or just tender. Drain well.

Melt the butter in a large saucepan. Add the onion and garlic and cook for 2 minutes, then add the noodles, tomatoes and parsley, and cook for a further 2–3 minutes, gently lifting and moving the pasta with a fork. Season to taste with salt and pepper. Serve at once in a heated earthenware dish or individual soup plates, sprinkled with a little grated cheese.

Vegetable frittata

Serves 2–3

Frittata *is an Italian flat omelette, very similar to the Spanish omelette often served as part of* tapas, *or pre-dinner nibbles with drinks. These are simple, easy and delicious, good to eat either hot or cold, and are infinite in their variety. The only thing to watch is not to overcook; they should be set but still slightly moist inside.*

Potatoes, cauliflower, red peppers, broccoli, peas, broad beans, onions, spinach, mushrooms, courgettes or left-over ratatouille are some of the vegetables you can use. Seasonings of garlic and fresh herbs can be added, as can Parmesan cheese or diced bacon or continental-style sausages and salamis, though beware of adding too many ingredients! The golden rule is to keep the toppings simple. As a rule of thumb, allow one egg and about 4 oz (100 g) cooked vegetables per person, plus an extra egg if the mixture is very thick. Ideal accompaniments are baked jacket potatoes and salads.

Lynda Brown

2 tablespoons olive or sunflower oil
8–10 oz (225–275 g) onion, thinly sliced
4 oz (100 g) broccoli or other green vegetables such as peas
3 eggs, lightly beaten
1 oz (25 g) Parmesan cheese (optional)
Salt and freshly ground black pepper (optional)
A knob of butter

Heat 1 teaspoon oil in a pan. Add the onions, cover and cook over a very low heat for a good 40 minutes until much reduced, stirring occasionally. During this time the onions mellow and become beautifully sweet, giving the frittata a lovely rich flavour. If you want, they can be cooked in advance, cooled and kept in a container in the refrigerator.

Meanwhile, quickly cook the green vegetables; do not overcook but keep them *al dente*, with a bite to them. Except for peas, chop the vegetables into bite-size pieces and mix with the eggs and onion mixture, stirring thoroughly. Add the Parmesan and seasoning, if using.

Heat the remaining oil with the butter in a frying-pan over moderate heat. Pour in the mixture and cook over a low heat for about 5–10 minutes until the underside is brown and the top almost done. Slip the pan under a moderate grill to set and brown the top. Serve at once, cut into wedges.

Risotto alla Bréscia

Serves 4

More like a thick broth than a standard risotto, this dish has beef marrow as an ingredient. Ask your butcher to chop a marrow bone (if you're lucky you might get it for free), place in a saucepan, cover with water and heat until the marrow is soft and can be scooped out with the end of a spoon. Serve this risotto with hot, crusty garlic bread and a green salad.

Shirley Goode

A knob of concentrated butter (see page 13)
1 large onion, grated
1 tablespoon fresh parsley, finely chopped
1–2 tablespoons beef marrow (see above)
1½ pints (900 ml) chicken stock
3 oz (75 g) frozen peas
8 oz (225 g) brown rice (dry weight), cooked
2 oz (50 g) hard cheese such as Cheddar, finely grated

Melt the butter in a large saucepan, add the onion and parsley and gently fry until the onion is softened but not coloured. Blend in the marrow, then add the stock and the peas and simmer for 10 minutes.

Stir in the rice and continue simmering for a further 3 minutes. Ladle into individual soup dishes and sprinkle the cheese over the tops. Serve hot.

Chunky vegetables with peanut dressing

Serves 4

This very versatile dressing can double as a dip if you make it with a little less water; using the full amount of liquid it becomes a thick coating sauce. Serve the dressing with lightly cooked chilled vegetables as a starter or with cold chicken for a main course.

Shirley Goode

2 lb (1 kg) evenly chopped cooked vegetables such as potatoes, celery, carrots and cauliflower
1 garlic clove, or 1 teaspoon garlic purée
1/2 teaspoon ground ginger
1 dessertspoon sunflower oil
3 tablespoons crunchy peanut butter
3 fl oz (85 ml) water
2 teaspoons honey
Juice of 1 lemon
Freshly ground black pepper
1–2 dessertspoons natural yoghurt
4 small hard-boiled eggs, quartered, to garnish

Put the garlic and ginger in a frying-pan, blend in the oil and fry for 2 minutes. Reduce heat to low, add the peanut butter and whisk in the water until well blended. Bring to the boil, then remove from heat. Stir in the honey and lemon juice and season to taste with black pepper. Put dressing in a bowl and set aside to cool.

Arrange the vegetables attractively on a large platter – they can be served hot, cold or at a room temperature.

When ready to serve, stir the yoghurt into the dressing, then pour the dressing over the vegetables. Garnish with the eggs.

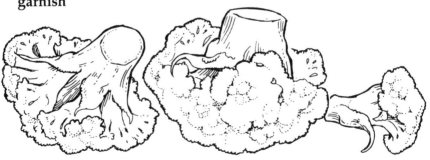

Forfar bridie

Serves 4

Here's Scotland's answer to Cornwall's culinary contribution – the pasty. This is simple to make, very substantial, inexpensive and has the advantage that you can make it in advance and refrigerate until required. Serve hot or cold with baked potatoes and a fresh chive and yoghurt dressing.

Make sure you use the left-over bits of pastry – these are ideal for turning into jam turnovers, simply by using the same method as below.

Kevin Woodford

12 oz (350 g) lean minced beef
3 oz (75 g) cooked chopped onion
1 teaspoon chopped fresh parsley
1 garlic clove, crushed
1/2 teaspoon dried mixed herbs
4 fl oz (120 ml) beef stock
Salt and freshly ground black pepper
12 oz (350 g) puff pastry, thawed if frozen
1 egg, beaten, to glaze

Pre-heat the oven to gas mark 4, 350°F (180°C).

Mix together the meat, onion, parsley, garlic and herbs, then moisten with the stock. Season to taste with salt and pepper.

Roll out the puff pastry on a lightly floured surface to 1/4 in (5 mm) thick and cut out 4 rounds, using a 6 in (15 cm) plate as a guide. Place a heap of the beef mixture on half of each round and wet the edges. Fold the empty half over the filled half and seal by pinching the 2 edges together.

Lightly brush with the egg, then bake for 20–25 minutes until golden brown.

Potato pizza

Serves 2

Potatoes are our most versatile vegetable, and certainly the one we never seem to tire of. This is a way of turning them into a main course, or a substantial snack, to enjoy when you get home late, or if you live on your own and cannot be bothered with elaborate dinners, but want something more appetising than convenience foods. For a single portion, use 8 oz (225 g) potato and 1 egg, size 3.

You can use various toppings for this dish – a little left-over chicken, strips of fried bacon, slices of salami, tuna fish, and so on – balancing the other ingredients and seasonings to suit.

Lynda Brown

1 lb (450 g) potatoes, peeled and coarsely grated
1 large egg, beaten
A pinch of salt
1–2 tablespoons olive or vegetable oil
Topping
2–3 tomatoes, sliced
2–3 oz (50–75 g) Cheddar or Lancashire cheese, crumbled or thinly sliced
A few stoned black olives, quartered
Dried oregano, or Italian seasoning

Place the potatoes in a bowl and mix with the egg and a pinch of salt. Heat enough of the oil to ensure an even coating in a large heavy based or non-stick frying-pan. When it is hot, tip in the potatoes; the mixture should sizzle slightly as it hits the pan. Press the mixture down with a fish slice and smooth the surface. Cook, undisturbed, over a gentle heat for 10–15 minutes.

Loosen the sides and base with a palette knife. Cover the pan with a large plate and invert so the potato pancake transfers to the plate, upside down. Use your oven gloves for this. Add a little more oil to the pan, and slide in the potato pancake, uncooked side down. (Alternatively, you can make two individual bases using two small pans. In this case, all you need to do is to loosen as before, slip the knife underneath the base and turn it over.)

Arrange the tomatoes over the surface, then top with the cheese. Scatter over the olives and a generous sprinkling of herbs, cover, then continue cooking gently for a further 10 minutes or until the cheese has melted and the tomatoes are hot. Ease out gently and serve.

Basic pizza dough

Makes 4 × 10 in (25 cm) thin crust pizzas, or 3 × 8 in (20 cm) deep-pan pizzas

To save time use easy-blend dried yeast (sometimes called easy-bake). This is dried yeast with vitamin C added to make it work faster. It's much easier to use than ordinary dried yeast – just stir it into the flour with the salt and sugar – and easier to get hold of than fresh yeast.

Gill MacLennan

12 oz (350 g) strong plain flour
1 teaspoon sugar
½ teaspoon salt
2 teaspoons easy-blend dried yeast
1 tablespoon vegetable oil
Extra flour for dusting
Sunflower oil for brushing

Place the flour, sugar, salt, yeast and oil in a large mixing bowl. Add 8 fl oz (250 ml) warm water and mix well with a knife to form a firm dough.

Knead the dough on a lightly floured work surface for 10 minutes until it becomes smooth and elastic. Place a little oil in a polythene bag and shake the bag well to coat. Add the dough and leave in a warm place for 30 minutes–1 hour until risen and doubled in size. Turn the dough out onto the floured work surface and knead for 5 minutes until smooth again.

Pre-heat the oven to gas mark 8, 450°F (230°C).

For thin crust pizzas
Flour 2 baking trays. Roll each piece of dough into a ball and flatten into 10 in (25 cm) rounds with a rolling pin.

69

Place the rounds on the baking trays. When topped, cook 2 at a time, then repeat.

For deep-pan pizzas
Flour 3 × 8 in (20 cm) round sandwich tins. Roll each piece of dough into a ball and flatten into each tin with your hands.

The bases are now ready for topping, see Four seasons pizza (opposite). Once topped, bake for 10 minutes for thin crust, or 15 minutes for deep-pan or until dough is well risen and golden brown.

Pizza topping sauce

Makes 5 fl oz (150 ml)

This is a thick, rich, red tomato sauce that's ideal for spreading over the pizza dough. It freezes well, in small polythene containers or in ice cube trays.

Gill MacLennan

1 small onion, chopped
1 garlic clove, chopped
1 × 14 oz (397 g) can tomatoes
3 tablespoons tomato purée
1 teaspoon dried oregano
Pinch of sugar
Salt and freshly ground black pepper

Place the onion and garlic in a small saucepan. Add tomatoes, tomato purée, oregano and sugar. Bring to the boil, reduce heat to a simmer and cook, uncovered, for 10 minutes, stirring occasionally, until the sauce is thickened and the onions soft. Remove from the heat, add salt and pepper to taste and spread over prepared pizza dough.

Four seasons pizza

Makes 3 deep-pan pizzas

This is a classic Italian pizza with a different topping on each quarter to represent spring, summer, autumn and winter.

Gill MacLennan

1 quantity of Basic pizza dough (page 69)
1 quantity of Pizza topping sauce (opposite)
1 large onion, sliced and fried until golden
½ small green pepper, de-seeded and chopped
18 capers, well drained
12 oz (350 g) Edam or mozzarella cheese, sliced
6 mushrooms, wiped and sliced
3 tomatoes, sliced
1 × 1¾ oz (42 g) can anchovy fillets, well drained
12 black stoned olives
Sunflower oil for brushing

Pre-heat the oven to gas mark 8, 450°F (230°C).
Cut the prepared dough into 3 portions and cut 2 small pieces from each piece and roll into thin sausage shapes. Flour 3 × 8 in (20 cm) round sandwich tins. Roll the 3 large pieces of dough into balls and flatten each into a tin with your hands.
   Spread each base with 3 tablespoons of the pizza topping sauce. Arrange the sausage shape strips of dough in a cross over sauce. In the first quarter put the fried onion, chopped pepper and capers; in the next quarter put half the sliced cheese and the sliced mushrooms; in the next quarter put the sliced tomato and the anchovies; in the remaining quarter put the remaining sliced cheese and the olives. Brush the mushrooms with oil.
   Bake for 15 minutes until well risen and golden. Serve at once.

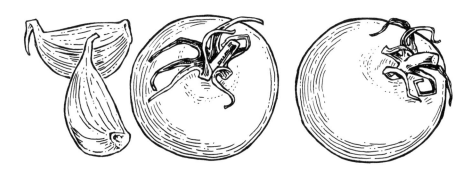

71

Spinach and cheese wholemeal quiche

The blend of cream cheese and spinach tantalises the taste-buds in this lovely recipe.

Kevin Woodford

Serves 4

8 oz (225 g) plain
  wholemeal flour
Pinch of salt
5 oz (150 g) butter or
  margarine, chilled
Filling
1 tablespoon sunflower
  oil
4 oz (100 g) onion,
  finely chopped
1 garlic clove, crushed
8 oz (225 g) frozen
  spinach, cooked,
  well drained and
  chopped, or 2 lb
  (900 g) fresh, cooked
  and chopped
1 egg, lightly beaten
4 oz (100 g) low-fat
  cream cheese
Pinch of ground
  cinnamon
Juice of ½ lemon
Salt and freshly ground
  black pepper
1 oz (25 g) Parmesan or
  Cheddar cheese,
  grated

To make the pastry, sieve the flour and salt into a bowl, adding any bran left in the sieve. Add the butter and rub in with fingertips until the mixture resembles breadcrumbs. Sprinkle over 2 tablespoons chilled water, and quickly mix to form a soft dough. Wrap in cling-film and chill for at least 30 minutes.

Pre-heat the oven to gas mark 4, 350°F (180°C). Lightly grease an 8 in (20 cm) flan tin.

To make the filling, heat the oil in a heavy based saucepan. Add the onion and garlic and cook for 2–3 minutes until softened but not browned. Add the spinach, egg and cheese and mix thoroughly together. Remove from the heat, then add the cinnamon and lemon juice. Season to taste with salt and pepper.

Roll out the pastry on a lightly floured surface and line the flan tin. Spoon the filling into the pastry shell and sprinkle the grated cheese over the top. Bake for 25 minutes or until set. Serve hot or at room temperature.

# Vegetables & salads

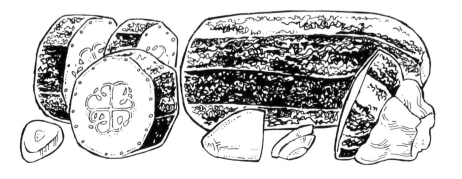

Red cabbage with apple

Serves 4

Served with grilled pork sausages or chops and mashed potatoes this dish is delicious. Once cooked it will keep for up to three days in the fridge – just heat through, stirring occasionally, to serve.

Gill MacLennan

**2 tablespoons sun-
flower oil
1 onion, sliced
1 lb (450 g) red cab-
bage, finely shredded
1 cooking apple,
peeled, cored and
coarsely chopped
2 tablespoons malt
vinegar
2 teaspoons unrefined
brown sugar
¼ teaspoon ground
cloves
Salt and freshly ground
black pepper**

Heat the oil in a large saucepan and fry the onion for 5 minutes until softened but not browned. Add the cabbage and the apple and cook, stirring, for 3–4 minutes. Add the vinegar, sugar, cloves, salt and pepper to taste and ½ pint (300 ml) water, then reduce the heat to simmering.

Cover the pan and simmer for 40 minutes, shaking the pan occasionally to stop the cabbage sticking. Stir well, then add more salt and pepper if desired and serve hot.

Sautéed courgettes and fennel with lemon and garlic

Serves 4

Though Florence fennel, those pale green-white bulbs tufted with feathery fronds, have become fairly common, they are still expensive. Raw, a little will go a long way in a salad, but the milder tenderness of cooked fennel can mean either a skimpy-looking portion, or an inflated grocery bill. In this recipe, however, one fennel bulb is stretched generously around four people by cooking it with courgettes, so the damage is minimised especially in the summer when courgettes are plentiful.

Sophie Grigson

1 large fennel bulb,
   woody stalk and
   base trimmed, and
   quartered
1 oz (25 g) butter
1 tablespoon sunflower
   oil
12 oz (350 g) courgettes,
   cut into ¹/₂ in
   (1 cm) slices
1 garlic clove, chopped
Grated zest of 1 lemon
Salt and freshly ground
   black pepper
2 teaspoons lemon juice

Cook the fennel in boiling lightly
salted water for 3 minutes. Drain well,
and thickly slice each quarter.
   Heat the butter and the oil in a large
frying-pan, then add the courgettes,
garlic and half the lemon zest. Sauté
for a few minutes until the courgettes
begin to soften, then add the fennel
and remaining lemon zest. Continue
sautéeing until the courgettes are
tender. Season well with salt and pepper and lemon juice. Serve at once.

Cauliflower fritters

Makes 12–16 fritters

This is one of those comfortable, welcome supper dishes that are immensely enjoyable, though they would never be seen gracing the menus of the grand restaurants. If you have enough, use left-over cauliflower – halve the quantities if necessary – as long as it isn't overcooked to a watery mush. For vegetarians or just for a change, substitute mushrooms cooked separately in a little extra butter or oil for the bacon.

Sophie Grigson

1 lb (450 g) cauliflower
   without leaves,
   broken into florets
4 eggs, separated
2 oz (50 g) bacon
   rashers, crisply
   cooked and
   crumbled
2 oz (50 g) plain flour
2 oz (50 g) fresh white
   breadcrumbs

Steam or boil the cauliflower until just
tender. Drain well, then mash with
the egg yolks. Mix in the bacon, flour
and breadcrumbs. Season to taste
with salt, cayenne and the nutmeg.
   Whisk the egg whites until stiff and
stir about one third into the
cauliflower mixture, then fold in the
remaining whites with a large metal
spoon. Heat about ¹/₂ in (1 cm) oil in a
large frying-pan. Drop generous

Salt
Cayenne pepper
1/4 teaspoon grated
  nutmeg
Sunflower oil for frying
Lemon wedges, to
  serve

spoonfuls of the mixture into the oil,
flattening them to a thickness of about
1/2 in (1 cm), and fry until golden
brown on both sides, turning once.
Continue until all the batter is used.
Drain well on kitchen paper and serve
hot with lemon wedges for squeezing
over the top.

Parsnip and potato gratin

Serves 4

*I'm always a sucker for baked potato
dishes. And that goes for parsnips, too.
Here they are baked with garlic – a sure
winner.*

Sophie Grigson

1 lb (450 g) parsnips,
  peeled and sliced
  about 1/4 in (5 mm)
  thick
1 lb (450 g) potatoes,
  peeled and sliced
  about 1/4 in (5 mm)
  thick
Salt and freshly ground
  black pepper
1–2 garlic cloves
2–3 oz (50–75 g) butter,
  or 3 tablespoons
  sunflower oil, or 1
  tablespoon walnut
  oil and 2 tablespoons
  sunflower oil

Pre-heat the oven to gas mark 6, 400°F
(200°C).
  Bring a large saucepan of lightly
salted water to the boil. Add the
parsnips, return to the boil, then
reduce heat to a simmer and cook for
4 minutes. Remove the parsnips with
a slotted spoon and drain well on
kitchen paper. Put the potato slices
into the same pan, return to the boil,
then reduce heat to a simmer and
cook for 3 minutes. Drain well.
  Grease a 9 in (23 cm) ovenproof
dish and spread a layer of potatoes on
the base. Sprinkle with salt and
pepper to taste and a little of the
garlic. Dot with butter or drizzle with
oil. Top with a layer of parsnips.
Sprinkle with salt and pepper to taste
and a little of the garlic. Dot with
butter or oil and repeat the layers
until all the vegetables are used. Dot
the upper surface with butter or oil.
Bake for 30 minutes.

Egyptian aubergine

Serves 4

This makes a wonderful first course, or is perfect as a main dish with a crisp green salad and some minted potatoes. It is equally good served as an unusual vegetable dish to accompany a main meat course.

The earthiness of the aubergines makes a good combination with the lamb but you can use minced beef if you prefer.

Kevin Woodford

2 aubergines, halved
    lengthways
2 fl oz (50 ml) sunflower
    oil
1 oz (25 g) onion,
    chopped
1 garlic clove, crushed
2 oz (50g) mushrooms,
    chopped
4 oz (100 g) cooked
    lamb, minced or
    finely chopped
Salt and freshly ground
    black pepper
2 tomatoes, sliced
1 teaspoon finely
    chopped fresh
    parsley

Pre-heat the oven to gas mark 4, 350°F (180°C).

Score the aubergine pulp criss-cross style. Heat 1 fl oz (25 ml) of the oil in a large frying-pan, add the aubergine halves and cook lightly. Drain well, and, using a spoon, scoop out the flesh, taking care not to pierce the shells. Finely chop the flesh and set aside.

Heat the remaining oil in a large frying-pan and add the onion, garlic and mushrooms. Cook for 3–4 minutes, stirring occasionally, until softened. Add the meat and aubergine flesh and mix thoroughly. Season to taste with salt and pepper. Fill the aubergine shells with the lamb mixture and top with tomato slices. Bake for 10–12 minutes until warmed through. Sprinkle with parsley and serve at once.

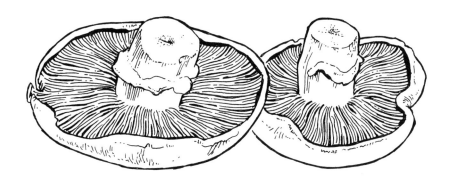

Cheesy 'baked' potato

Serves 1

If you cook baked potatoes in a microwave they don't have that crispy skin you get if you bake them in a conventional oven but they are ready so much more quickly.

Gill MacLennan

1 large potato, about 8 oz (225 g)
2 oz (50 g) mature Cheddar cheese, grated
Salt and freshly ground black pepper
1 tablespoon thick Greek yoghurt

Prick the potato all over with a fork. Microwave on High (100%) for 8 minutes, or bake at gas mark 6, 400°F (200°C) for 1–1½ hours.
  Meanwhile, mix the cheese with the salt and pepper to taste and the yoghurt. Cut a deep cross in the top of the potato, and squeeze the sides to open the top. Spoon in the cheesy filling and eat at once while still hot.

Frozen oven chips

Makes about 5 lb (2.25 kg)

It's easy and much cheaper to make these yourself than to buy the commercial variety, if somewhat time-consuming. Buy a big bag of potatoes and do them in a batch to make it worth your while. Ask your greengrocer for the best chipping potato as they vary depending on the time of the year. Maris pipers and Majestics are good.

Gill MacLennan

5 lb (2.25 kg) potatoes
Sunflower oil

Peel the potatoes into a large bowl of cold salted water. Cut into slices ¼ in (5 mm) thick, then into lengths. Return to the bowl until ready to cook to stop potatoes turning brown.
  Remove some of the chips from the bowl and pat dry on kitchen paper or between 2 tea towels. Half-fill a deep-fat pan with oil and pre-heat to 375°F (190°C) or until a piece of potato dropped gently into the oil rises to the

surface immediately surrounded by bubbles. Quarter fill the chip basket and fry the potatoes for 3–4 minutes until softened but not coloured. Lift the basket over the pan, shake off the excess oil and tip the chips onto a baking tray lined with kitchen paper, then leave to cool. Repeat with remaining potatoes.

Remove the kitchen paper and spread the chips out on baking trays. Open freeze for 3 hours or until solid. Place in polythene bags in handy portions, seal, label and freeze flat. Use within 3 months.

To cook from frozen, pre-heat the oven to gas mark 8, 450°F (230°C). Shake the frozen chips onto a baking tray and spread out evenly. Cook for 15–20 minutes until golden brown. Serve at once.

Potato pancakes

Makes 12 pancakes

These delicious pancakes can be served with salad as a light lunch dish or as an accompaniment to a main dish. They are ideal for Bonfire Night parties.

Elisabeth Allen, Stanford le Hope

2 large potatoes, peeled and grated
1 large onion, peeled and grated
1 egg
3 tablespoons plain flour
Salt and pepper to taste
Sunflower oil

Mix all the ingredients together except the oil. Heat a little oil in a frying-pan and drop in 3 separate tablespoons of the mixture. Flatten them slightly to form cakes. When golden on the underside, turn and fry the other sides until golden. Turn out onto a warm plate and keep hot. Fry the rest of the mixture in batches. Serve as soon as possible.

Potato and pepper tortilla

Serves 6–8

Cooking the potatoes and onions in olive oil for this Spanish omelette gives the best, slightly smoky flavour. You could, I suppose, just boil the potatoes, and fry the onions in one tablespoon of oil. Fewer calories, still nice, but it will never taste as special, or as Spanish.

Sophie Grigson

3 large potatoes, peeled and thinly sliced
1 large onion, thinly sliced
2¹/₂–5 fl oz (65–150 ml) olive oil
2¹/₂–5 fl oz (65–150 ml) sunflower oil
1 red pepper
1 green pepper
6 eggs, beaten
Salt

Layer the potatoes and onions in a large frying-pan and pour in enough oil to just cover, using half olive and half grapeseed oil. Cover and cook over a gentle heat, turning the slices occasionally to make sure they cook evenly and do not stick together.

When tender, drain off the oil and reserve for later use. Set aside the potato and onion slices to cool.

Meanwhile, grill the peppers until black and blistered all over. Drop into a polythene bag and seal. Set aside until cool enough to handle, then skin, remove the seeds and cut into strips about 2 in (5 cm) long and ¹/₂ in (1 cm) wide.

Add the potatoes, onions and salt to the eggs. Mix well and set aside for 15 minutes for flavours to mingle. Stir in the peppers.

Heat 3 tablespoons of the reserved oil in a frying-pan large enough to take all the ingredients in a single layer 1–1¹/₂ in (2.5–4 cm) thick. When it is very hot, tip in all the egg mixture and smooth the surface, pushing it down slightly. Cook until sides are crusty and brown and the tortilla is thickening in the middle. Place the pan under a hot grill and brown the top. Turn out onto a serving dish and serve tepid or cold.

Pasta with tomato sauce

Serves 2–3 over pasta

This tomato sauce can be poured over any kind of piping hot pasta and sprinkled with freshly grated Parmesan cheese for a simple, quick meal. Add extra ingredients, such as thawed frozen peas, green beans, chillies, ham strips, bacon or salami, red or green peppers and mushrooms fried in a little extra oil and you can create a seemingly infinite number of variations.

The carrot and celery are not absolutely necessary, but they do add extra flavour and substance to the sauce.

Sophie Grigson

1 tablespoon olive or sunflower oil
1 onion, chopped
2 garlic cloves, chopped
1 carrot, finely chopped
1 celery stick, finely chopped
1 × 14 oz (397 g) can tomatoes, chopped, or 1 lb (450 g) fresh tomatoes, skinned and coarsely chopped
1 tablespoon chopped fresh basil, or ¹/₂ teaspoon dried marjoram
¹/₂ teaspoon sugar
Dash of red wine vinegar
1 tablespoon tomato paste
Salt and freshly ground black pepper
4 oz (100 g) dried pasta per person

Heat the oil in a large pan. Add the onion, garlic, carrot and celery and gently cook until the onion is softened. Add the remaining sauce ingredients and simmer until the sauce is thick and pulpy, with no trace of wateriness. Taste and adjust the seasoning. Use as it is, or purée to give a smoother sauce. Keep warm.

To cook the pasta, bring a very large pan of salted water to the boil. Add a tablespoon of oil to the water, then add the pasta in a slow steady stream, so that the water barely goes off the boil. Check cooking time on the packet – about a minute before this time is up, start testing the pasta. As soon as it is al dente, that is tender, but still slightly resistant to the bite, drain well, and return to the hot pan. Add a drizzle of oil, and toss well. Serve immediately, topped with the sauce.

NOTE: To make a simple tomato soup, purée with chicken or vegetable stock, and re-heat with fresh herbs and a swirl of cream or natural yoghurt.

Moroccan orange and carrot salad

Serves 4 as a side salad

A simple and refreshing salad, good either in winter or summer. Orange flower water, available from chemists' shops, was a favourite ingredient well into the nine-teenth century in English cookery. It was at one time used frequently in savoury dishes as well as sweets and desserts. It has a lovely perfumed flavour and you need very little. Use it by the teaspoon, adding it cautiously. Try it in fruit salads, custards or in cake fillings, as well as this unusual salad.

Lynda Brown

1 orange, carefully peeled and thinly sliced with all pips removed
8–10 oz (225–275 g) carrot, grated
Dressing
Juice of ½ lemon
1 dessertspoon sugar
1 teaspoon orange flower water

Very lightly mix the orange with the carrot in a salad bowl. Stir all the dressing ingredients together until the sugar has dissolved, then pour over the salad. Cover until ready to serve.

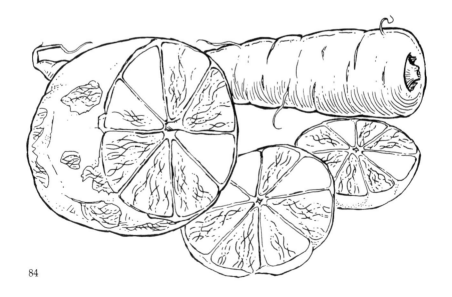

Peasant salad

Serves 4

The French term for this salad is salade tiède *which literally means 'a warm salad'. Serve it as a first course or a main dish, along with some hot crusty bread.*

Lesley Waters

1 Cos lettuce, leaves
separated
8 oz (225 g) fresh spin-
ach, trimmed, leaves
separated and rinsed
2 tablespoons sun-
flower oil
3 streaky bacon rash-
ers, rinded and diced
2 thick slices whole-
meal bread, cubed
2 hard boiled eggs,
coarsely chopped
1 garlic clove, crushed
3 oz (75 g) left-over
Stilton or Cheddar
cheese, crumbled
Dressing
Grated rind and juice
of 1 lemon
4 tablespoons sun-
flower oil
1 teaspoon French
mustard
1 tablespoon finely
chopped fresh
parsley
Salt and freshly ground
black pepper

To make the dressing, mix all the ingredients together and season to taste
with salt and pepper. Set aside until
required.

Heat 2 tablespoons oil in a frying-
pan and gently fry the bacon until
lightly browned. Add the bread cubes
and continue frying until the croûtons
are golden brown. Remove from the
pan, drain on kitchen paper and
crumble the bacon pieces.

Toss the salad leaves with the eggs,
bacon and croûtons in a large salad
bowl. Pour the dressing into the
frying-pan and bring to the boil. Add
the garlic and cook for 1 minute,
stirring, then pour over the salad and
toss again. Sprinkle the cheese on top
and serve at once.

Hot omelette salad

Serves 4

This is an excellent lunch or supper dish. Serve with hot buttered toast or with warm wholemeal bread.

Lesley Waters

4 eggs
2 tablespoons water or milk
Salt and freshly ground black pepper
A knob of butter
1 Cos lettuce, or a selection of salad leaves
2 oz (50 g) mature Cheddar cheese, grated
Dressing
1 tablespoon white wine vinegar
5 tablespoons sunflower oil
1 garlic clove, crushed
1 teaspoon prepared mustard
1 tablespoon chopped fresh parsley

Whisk the eggs until well mixed, then add the water and salt and pepper to taste. Melt the butter in an omelette pan or frying-pan. Add the eggs and gently stir with a fork, drawing in the liquid from the sides to the centre. When the eggs are set, stop stirring and cook for about 1 minute until golden on the bottom. Remove from the heat. Place a plate over the pan and invert so the omelette falls out of the pan. Slide back into the pan, cooked side up, and cook for 30 seconds–1 minute until golden and set on the other side. Set aside and keep warm.

To make the dressing, combine all the ingredients in a bowl, season to taste with salt and pepper and whisk well.

Tear the lettuce into small pieces and place in a salad bowl. Pour over the dressing and toss. Cut the omelette into noodle-like strips and add to the salad while still hot with the cheese. Lightly toss again and serve straight away.

Desserts and puddings

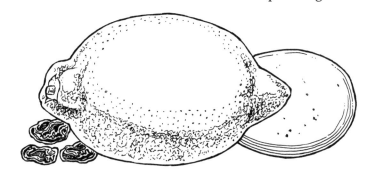

Hot chocolate soufflé with white chocolate sauce

Serves 6

This, I have to confess, isn't a budget recipe at all – but it is wonderful and not nearly as difficult as it sounds. The stunning colour combination of a dark chocolate soufflé with a white sauce makes this a really impressive pudding, and the flavours are beautiful. The art of good soufflé-making is in the serving – it will not wait until you are ready, so be sure you concentrate on timing. Don't be afraid to make your guests wait while you prepare and bake the soufflé. The whole process only takes about 20 minutes – well worth waiting for. It helps if you make the sauce in advance and keep it warm in the top half of a double boiler.

Kevin Woodford

1 oz (25 g) butter, plus extra for greasing
Plain flour for dusting
6 oz (175 g) plain chocolate, broken into pieces
3 eggs, separated
1 tablespoon dark rum
2 extra egg whites
1 oz (25 g) sugar
Sauce
2 oz (50 g) butter
2 oz (50 g) plain flour
1 pint (600 ml) hot milk
4 oz (100 g) white chocolate, broken into pieces
1¹/₂ oz (40 g) sugar

Pre-heat the oven to gas mark 4, 350°F (180°C). Grease and lightly dust 6 ramekin dishes (5 fl oz (150 ml) in size) with flour, then place in the refrigerator.

Melt the chocolate in the top half of a double boiler, then stir in 1 oz (25 g) butter. Whisk in the egg yolks and rum, whisking constantly. Remove from the heat, set aside to cool slightly: if it cools too much, it will set because of the chocolate. Whisk all the egg whites and sugar together until stiff, then fold into the chocolate mixture using a large metal spoon. Remove the ramekins from the refrigerator and fill to ¹/₂ in (1 cm) from the top with the chocolate mixture. Bake for 8–10 minutes, until well risen. Serve at once.

To make the sauce, melt the butter in a heavy-based saucepan, add the flour and stir to mix, cooking for 2–3

89

minutes. Gradually add the hot milk, stirring constantly. Add the chocolate with the sugar and mix thoroughly to dissolve the chocolate. Serve hot in a sauceboat for spooning over the soufflés.

Chocolate Pavlova

Serves 6

This makes a great change from the normal vanilla version. You can make one 8 in (20 cm) Pavlova or 6 individual nests and, if you prefer, use chocolate ice-cream instead of cream for the filling.

Lesley Waters

5 egg whites
Pinch of salt
10 oz (275 g) caster
  sugar
1½ oz (40 g) cocoa
  powder
1½ oz (40 g) granulated
  sugar
1 tablespoon cornflour
2 teaspoons lemon
  juice
Filling
3 large oranges
10 fl oz (300 ml)
  whipping cream,
  whipped

Pre-heat the oven to gas mark 1, 275°F (140°C).

Place a sheet of aluminium foil on a baking tray and lightly grease. Draw an 8 in (20 cm) circle or oval on the foil, or 6 smaller circles/ovals.

Beat the egg whites and salt until stiff, then add the caster sugar, 1 tablespoon at a time, and continue beating for 10 minutes.

In a separate bowl, mix together the cocoa powder, granulated sugar and cornflour. Fold this mixture and the lemon juice into the meringue with a large metal spoon. Spoon the meringue mixture over the circle(s) or oval(s). Bake in the middle of the oven for 2 hours. Turn off the heat and leave the meringue to cool slowly with the oven door closed.

To make the filling, grate the orange zest and stir into the whipped cream. Spoon the cream onto the cooled meringue. Peel the oranges with a sharp knife, removing all the pith. Slice the oranges and arrange on top. Chill until ready to serve.

Apricot and lime fool

Makes 4

I wouldn't go as far as to claim this is a positively cheap or health-promoting pudding but it isn't nearly as wickedly indulgent as it tastes. For a start, there's plenty of fibre from the apricots, and then the combination of half whipped cream and half fromage frais or natural yoghurt gives richness without quite as much fat as the traditional all-cream fruit fool has. Look out for ready-to-eat dried apricots that don't require any soaking.

Sophie Grigson

6 oz (175 g) dried apricots
Grated zest and juice of 1½ limes, or 1 lemon
2 oz (50 g) caster sugar
5 tablespoons whipping cream
5 tablespoons 8% fat fromage frais, or low-fat natural yoghurt

Soak the apricots according to the instructions on the packet if necessary. Place the apricots in a small pan and cover with cold water. Bring to the boil, reduce heat to a simmer and cook until the apricots are very tender. Purée or mash the apricots with the lime or lemon juice, sugar and enough of their cooking water to give a thick purée. Set aside to cool.

Whip the cream until it is stiff, then fold it into the apricot purée with the fromage frais and two thirds of the zest. Taste and add more sugar or juice if necessary. Divide between 4 glasses and sprinkle each with the remaining zest before serving. Cover with cling-film and chill until ready to serve.

Exotic hot fruit salad

Serves 4

Here's an exciting change from the 'run of the mill' fruit salad. Shortbread and whipped cream are ideal accompaniments. Chinese five-spice powder is available from larger supermarkets and oriental shops.

Lesley Waters

1 × 10 oz (275 g) can
lychees, drained
with syrup reserved
2 bananas, thickly
sliced
8 oz (225 g) plums,
stoned and sliced
8 oz (225 g) straw-
berries, hulled, or
other soft fruit in
season
2 oz (50 g) light brown
sugar
Grated zest and juice
of 1 lemon
1/2 teaspoon Chinese
five-spice powder
1 bay leaf
1 teaspoon fresh root
ginger, finely
chopped
8 fl oz (250 ml) apple
juice
3 tablespoons brandy
(optional)
1 tablespoon finely
chopped fresh mint

Pre-heat the oven to gas mark 5, 375°F (190°C).

Place all the prepared fruit in a large casserole. Combine the sugar with the lemon zest and juice, Chinese spices, bay leaf, ginger, apple juice, brandy and lychee syrup. Pour over the fruit, cover and bake for 20–30 minutes until bubbling hot. Stir in the mint and serve at once.

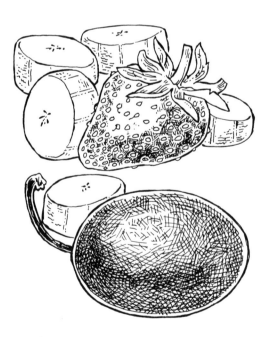

Cinnamon bananas

Serves 4

This is an excellent pudding, especially for cold winter days.

Lesley Waters

2 oz (50 g) butter
2 oz (50 g) dark brown
 sugar
Grated nutmeg
1 tablespoon ground
 cinnamon
Grated zest and juice
 of 2 large oranges
4 small bananas,
 peeled and halved
 lengthways
2 tablespoons whisky
 or dark rum (optional)
Greek yoghurt or
 whipped cream, to
 serve

Melt the butter and brown sugar in a large frying-pan. Add the nutmeg, cinnamon and orange zest and juice, then bring to the boil.
 Place the bananas in the syrup, cover and gently simmer for 5 minutes. Spoon over the whisky and flambé if desired. Serve hot with thick Greek yoghurt or whipped cream.

Mrs Beeton's cheap blancmange

Serves 4

This is a recipe from Mrs Beeton's cookery book, first published in 1861. It's a creamy delicate blancmange, lovely with summer fruits or a fruit purée, or on its own. Coming back to real blancmange again makes you realise what we have been missing all these years. In 1861, incidentally, this cost 4d to make.

Gelatine has too strong a taste for this delicate blancmange, so I use another gelling agent, agar-agar, which is both colourless and tasteless. It can be bought from chemists' shops or health food shops, and you use it the same way as gelatine. It is very useful for low-sugar jams too.

Lynda Brown

1 pint (600 ml) milk
2 bay leaves
2 thin strips thinly
  pared lemon zest
2 tablespoons agar-agar
  flakes, or 1 table-
  spoon granules
1–2 dessertspoons
  sugar

Put the milk and flavourings into a saucepan, sprinkle over the agar-agar, stir and slowly bring to simmering point. Allow to infuse over the lowest heat for about 10 minutes or until the milk is well flavoured.

Remove the bay leaves and lemon zest, then strain through a sieve, pressing hard to push through any remaining globules of agar-agar. Sweeten to taste, pour into individual dishes and set aside until set. Mrs Beeton suggested: 'garnish with preserves, bright jelly or a compote of fruit'.

Floating islands

Serves 4

Here is a simple pudding with plenty of appeal. The basic egg custard can be served plain or given additional flavour with a spoonful of instant chocolate or coffee stirred into the milk. For an optional garnish, drizzle melted chocolate over the meringues.

By poaching the meringues in hot water instead of the milk you don't have to make them at the same time as the custard, and the hot water can be used to wash the dishes! If you want to poach the meringues in the milk, however, prepare the meringue mixture first.

Shirley Goode

2 teaspoons cornflour
1 pint (600 ml) milk
A few drops of vanilla
  essence
3 eggs, separated
8 oz (225 g) caster sugar
2 oz cooking chocolate
  (optional)

Blend the cornflour with a little of the milk to make a smooth paste. Put the remaining milk into a saucepan with the vanilla and heat to the simmering point (the meringues can be poached in the milk at this point if you wish). Pour this mixture onto the cornflour mixture, then return to the heat, stirring constantly, until slightly thickened.

Beat the egg yolks with 2 oz (50 g) of the sugar until light and fluffy, then stir into the hot milk. Keep stirring for 1 minute until the custard is thick enough to coat the back of a spoon. Pour the custard into a serving bowl, cover with cling-film to prevent a skin forming and set aside to cool.

To make the meringues, heat a large pan of water to the simmering point but not boiling. Whisk the egg whites until soft peaks form, then whisk in half the remaining sugar and whisk again until stiff. Fold in the remaining sugar using a metal spoon.

Using a dessertspoon dipped in the hot water, scoop out several spoonfuls of meringue and gently drop each into the hot water. Poach for 1–2 minutes, then turn the meringues over and poach the other sides for a further 1 minute. Lift out with a slotted spoon and drain well on a cloth laid over a wire rack.

To serve, pile the meringues on top of the custard. Put the cooking chocolate, if using, in a small polythene bag and stand the bag in hot water until the chocolate has melted. Remove the bag from the water and twist to make a 'piping bag'. Either cut a tiny piece off the corner of the bag or pierce with a cocktail stick. Holding the bag over the meringues squeeze gently and drizzle the chocolate over the pudding to decorate. (If there is any chocolate left in the bag, put it in the ice compartment of the fridge to use again another day.)

Ecclefechan butter tart

Serves 6

This is a traditional Scottish open tart with a nutty wholemeal pastry and a butterscotch flavoured fruit and nut middle. Look out for walnut pieces when you're shopping – they're cheaper than walnut halves.

Gill MacLennan

6 oz (175 g) wholemeal shortcrust pastry
4 oz (100 g) butter
4 oz (100 g) light muscovado or soft brown sugar
1 tablespoon malt vinegar
2 eggs, size 3, well beaten
8 oz (225 g) mixed dried fruit
2 oz (50 g) walnut pieces

Pre-heat the oven to gas mark 5, 375°F (190°C).

Roll out the pastry on a lightly floured surface and use to line a 10 in (25 cm) ovenproof dinner plate or fluted flan tin.

Cream the butter and sugar together until light and fluffy, then beat in the vinegar. Gradually beat in the eggs and stir in the dried fruit and walnuts. Spread over the pastry base, levelling the top with the back of a spoon.

Place the tart on a baking tray and bake for 25 minutes until filling is golden. Serve warm or at room temperature.

Pumpkin pie

Makes a 9 in (23 cm) pie

If you're into pumpkin lanterns for Hallowe'en, then you'll be glad of more than one recipe to use up the scooped out flesh (see also Couscous, page 60).

To cook the pumpkin for this pie, put the cubed pumpkin flesh in a heatproof bowl with a very little water and cover tightly with foil. Bake in the oven at gas mark 3, 325°F (160°C) for about 30 minutes, or until the flesh is tender. Mash to a purée, then cook in a saucepan over a low heat until very thick. Cool before using. (This will freeze for up to one year.)

Shirley Goode

10 fl oz (300 ml) cooked pumpkin (see above)
2 eggs, separated
3 oz (75 g) light brown sugar
¼ teaspoon *each* ground cinnamon, ginger and grated nutmeg
5 fl oz (150 ml) milk
9 in (23 cm) uncooked shortcrust pie shell, thawed if frozen
Whipped cream, to serve (optional)

Pre-heat the oven to gas mark 5, 375°F (190°C).

Beat together the pumpkin, egg yolks, sugar and spices, then stir in the milk. Beat the egg whites until stiff, then fold into the pumpkin mixture with a large metal spoon. Pour into the pie shell and bake for 40 minutes or until set. Cool on a wire rack. Serve cold with whipped cream.

Chocolate and coffee torte

Serves 6–8

Every now and then I like to indulge in something really greedy. When I get the urge, this is my favourite pudding – just a small portion, though!

Kevin Woodford

3 oz (75 g) butter
3 oz (75 g) caster sugar
1 small glass sweet
  sherry
2 oz (50 g) cocoa
2 oz (50 g) walnut
  pieces
32 sponge fingers
5 fl oz (150 ml) hot
  black coffee
5 fl oz (150 ml)
  whipping cream
1/2 oz (15 g) coffee
  beans, to decorate
  (optional)
1/2 oz (15 g) whole
  walnuts, to decorate
  (optional)

Line an 8 in (20 cm) loose-bottomed flan ring or cake tin with aluminium foil.

Cream the butter and sugar together until light and fluffy, then stir in the sherry, cocoa and walnuts. The mixture should be light enough to spread easily; if not, add a little more sherry.

Lay half the sponge fingers, sugar side up, in the flan ring and thoroughly dampen with half the coffee. Cover the soaked biscuits completely with half the chocolate mix, then lay another layer of biscuits on top. Carefully dampen each biscuit with the remaining coffee using a large spoon, then cover with the remainder of the filling. Smooth the surface. Chill, preferably overnight, until set.

Just before serving, whip the cream until thickened but still spreadable. Remove the torte from the tin and cover the top and sides with the cream. Decorate with coffee beans and walnuts.

Lemon sorbet

Makes about 1³/₄ pints
(1 litre)

An easy way to remember basic sorbet proportions is 1 lb (450 g) sugar, plus 1 pint (600 ml) water, plus 1 pint (600 ml) fruit purée. The purée can be any sieved soft fruit. Basically all that has to be done to make a sorbet is to heat the water and sugar together until the sugar dissolves, then cool and stir in the fruit purée. Freeze the mixture in freezerproof containers with covers for 30 minutes, then stir the frozen sides to the middle and beat well. Repeat twice. You can either then solid freeze as it is for a 'sherbet', or finally fold in one or two beaten egg whites to make a 'sorbet' and then freeze. Here is a slightly different version using lemons:

Shirley Goode

8 oz (225 g) sugar
1 pint (600 ml) water
Grated zest and juice
   of 3 large lemons
2 egg whites

Place the sugar and water in a large saucepan, stirring to dissolve the sugar, and boil for 4 minutes. Stir in the grated lemon zest, then remove from the heat and set aside to cool.
   Stir in the lemon juice. Transfer to a freezerproof container, cover and freeze for 30 minutes or until frozen around the edges. Beat well until almost liquid. Whisk the egg whites until stiff, then fold into the sorbet mixture. Return to the container and freeze until solid. Remove from the freezer 5–10 minutes to soften before serving.

Warm English cheese on parkin with yoghurt dressing

I find very exciting the idea of combining good English cheese with a spicy parkin, even more so when highlighted with yoghurt and chives. This is ideal as a snack or to finish off a meal.

Remember, parkin is like a good cook – it improves with age, so make enough to store for a rainy day. For this dish it is best to leave the parkin for at least one week. Store in a cool place and make sure the parkin is well covered.

Kevin Woodford

4 oz (100 g) self-raising flour
4 oz (100 g) medium oatmeal
4 oz (100 g) soft light brown sugar
2 teaspoons ground ginger
1 egg, beaten
4 oz (100 g) black treacle
2 oz (50 g) sunflower margarine
5 tablespoons milk
2 oz (50 g) English cheese per person, sliced no more than ¹/₂ in (1 cm) thick
Lettuce leaves, to garnish
Yoghurt dressing
4 fl oz (120 ml) natural yoghurt
1 oz (25 g) fresh chives, snipped
¹/₂ teaspoon ground paprika
Ground black pepper

Pre-heat the oven to gas mark 4, 350°F (180°C). Line a 9 in (23 cm) square tin with greaseproof paper.

Place all the dry ingredients into a large bowl and beat in the egg. Warm the treacle, margarine and milk together. Pour the dry ingredients into the warm syrup and mix well together. Pour into the tin. Bake for 45–50 minutes or until a toothpick inserted in the centre comes out clean.

Meanwhile, make the dressing. Combine the yoghurt and chives and mix in the paprika and pepper to taste.

When the parkin is baked, cut pieces that are the same shape as the cheese slices. Place a piece of cheese on top of each piece of parkin. Put on the grill rack and grill 2–3 minutes, until melted and lightly brown. Serve surrounded by green leaves tossed in the dressing.

Cabinet pudding

Serves 4 to 6

This delightful pudding offers versatility in that it is just as delicious hot as cold. I like to make double the recipe so that we can enjoy a helping served straight from the oven (with a spoonful of ice-cream melting over it) and save a helping to serve cold later.

Kevin Woodford

4 oz (100 g) sponge cake or sponge fingers
1 oz (25 g) currants
1 pint (600 ml) milk
2 oz (50 g) caster sugar
4 eggs
2 drops vanilla essence

Pre-heat the oven to gas mark 5, 375°F (190°C).

Cut the cake into ¼ in (5 mm) dice, mix it with the currants and half-fill 4–6 small greased moulds with the mixture. Ramekins or dariole moulds are traditionally used but any small oven-proof dishes will do.

Warm the milk and sugar gently together in a pan, then whisk this into the eggs and vanilla essence and strain the entire mixture into a jug. Pour the strained mixture into the moulds until they are full to the top. Place them in a roasting tin that you have half-filled with water and leave them to stand for 10–15 minutes.

Cook the puddings in the oven for 35–40 minutes, then remove them and, again, leave them to stand for a few minutes. (This ensures they set.)

To serve hot, gently loosen each little pudding round the edge with a knife and turn the mould over onto a plate. Shake the mould gently and the pudding should slide out.

To serve cold, let the puddings cool in the moulds and refrigerate. Turn them out, as described above, when you need them.

Autumn pudding

Serves 4

Based on the traditional summer pudding recipe, this dessert uses cake instead of bread and makes the most of hedgerow and windfall fruit.

Shirley Goode

9 in (23 cm) square or round sponge cake
10 fl oz (300 ml) stewed blackberries
5 fl oz (150 ml) stewed apples
Fromage frais or natural yoghurt to serve

Split the sponge cake horizontally into 2 halves. Cut a small round from one half to fit the bottom of a 1½ pint (900 ml) pudding basin and a large round from the other half to fit the top.

Lay the small sponge round on the base of the basin, top with half the blackberries and cover with crumbled sponge trimmings. Add a layer of apples, more sponge trimmings and the remaining blackberries. Top with the large sponge round. Cover with a plate and a weight such as a can of beans and leave in a cold place overnight.

To serve, turn out onto a lipped, shallow dish and serve with fromage frais or yoghurt.

Apple and date pudding

Serves 4

This is a cake-like pudding, light but satisfying. Eating apples which can be picked up cheaply are often a better choice for such puddings than cookers. They keep their shape better and require far less sugar. Dried fruit is another natural sweetener with the double bonus of being richly flavoured and full to bursting with vitamins, minerals and fibre. The two together make a lovely winter pudding.

Lynda Brown

12 oz (350 g) eating apples, peeled, cored and thinly sliced
2 oz (50 g) dried dates, coarsely chopped
Finely grated zest of ½ lemon
2 oz (50 g) light soft brown sugar
2 oz (50 g) sunflower margarine
1 egg, lightly beaten
2 oz (50 g) self-raising flour
1 oz (25 g) fine oatmeal
1 teaspoon ground cinnamon (optional)
2 tablespoons milk

Pre-heat the oven to gas mark 5, 375°F (190°C).

Scatter the apples, three quarters of the dates and the lemon zest over the bottom of an ovenproof serving dish (a Pyrex rice pudding dish is ideal) and set aside.

Cream the sugar and margarine until light and fluffy, then beat in the egg, a little at a time. Sift the flour, oatmeal and cinnamon if using, then fold into the creamed mixture, stirring in enough milk to give a soft dropping consistency. Spoon the mixture over the fruit and scatter the remaining dates on top. Bake for about 40 minutes or until the centre is set.

Mama's lockshen pudding

Serves 6–8 (or just me!)

As the title suggests, this recipe is my mother's and, as a child, the fantastic aroma when it was baking in the oven used to drive me mad. Even today there's never much left over when I get at the dish.

Phil Diamond

12 oz (350 g) fine vermicelli
4 oz (100 g) raisins
2 oz (50 g) sugar
4 oz (100 g) lemon curd
2 eggs
Juice and finely grated zest of 1 lemon

Pre-heat the oven to gas mark 4, 350°F (180°C).

Put the vermicelli in a large saucepan of boiling water and cook until *al dente* or just tender, then drain well. Return the vermicelli to the saucepan, adding the remaining ingredients, and mix well. Grease an 8 × 8 × 2 in (20 × 20 × 5 cm) ovenproof dish and pour in the noodle mixture. Bake for 45 minutes or until golden brown on top. Serve hot or cold as pudding or a cake.

Baking

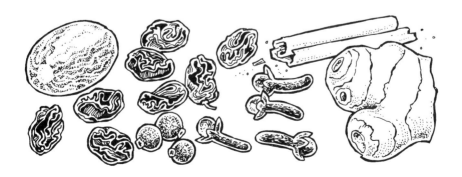

Wholemeal carrot scones

Makes 4 large triangles

Ever since carrot cake, or Passion cake, became popular, I've been grating carrots into all sorts of baked goods. In scones they add crunch and colour. I make these quickly in a round tin. They are delicious split and buttered straight from the oven, or cooled and filled with salad and cottage cheese for lunch.

Gill MacLennan

**8 oz (225 g) plain wholemeal flour
4 teaspoons baking powder
¹/₂ teaspoon salt
2 oz (50 g) margarine
1 carrot, scraped and coarsely grated
5 fl oz (150 ml) milk, to mix**

Pre-heat the oven to gas mark 6, 400°F (200°C).

Place the flour, baking powder and salt in a bowl. Rub in the margarine until the mixture resembles bread-crumbs. Stir in the carrot and mix well. Add the milk and mix to a fairly firm dough with a flat bladed knife. Lightly flour the work surface and knead the dough lightly.

Lightly grease a 7 in (18 cm) round sandwich tin and coat with whole-meal flour. Turn the dough into the tin and knead it lightly to smooth the top. Mark 4 triangles with a knife but don't cut through.

Bake for 20–25 minutes or until well risen and golden. Loosen the scone from the tin and turn out onto a wire rack. Pull the triangles apart to serve.

Spiced sticky tea buns

Makes about 10

These are a hot favourite in my household. They are based on a seventeenth-century recipe for a 'Great Cake or Fruit Loaf' in Hilary Spurling's book, Elinor Fettiplace's Receipt Book, *about one of her ancestors, Elinor Fettiplace, whose recipes have been handed down through the generations.*

The exact mixture of the spices can be altered to suit; if you do not have them separately, use ¹/₂ teaspoon ground allspice and cloves and 1 teaspoon grated nutmeg. Grinding your own spices in a coffee grinder gives the best results and produces a heavenly fragrance in the kitchen.

Lynda Brown

3 or 4 whole cloves
1 in (2.5 cm) piece cinnamon
3 or 4 allspice berries
¹/₂ teaspoon ground ginger
1 teaspoon freshly grated nutmeg
1 lb (450 g) strong white bread flour, or unbleached plain household flour
¹/₂ oz (15 g) fresh yeast, or ¹/₄ oz (10 g) dried
1 teaspoon sugar
¹/₂ pint (300 ml) milk, or ¹/₄ pint (150 ml) each of milk and dark brown ale
1 oz (25 g) butter
3 oz (75 g) currants or sultanas
1 oz (25 g) sugar
1 teaspoon rosewater (optional)

If using whole spices, grind them in a coffee grinder until reduced to a power. Mix all the spices with the flour in a large bowl and put in a low oven to warm through for a few minutes.

Meanwhile, cream the yeast with a little of the milk and sugar until dissolved. If using dried yeast, sprinkle over the warmed milk and sugar, mix in and set aside 10–15 minutes until frothy. Warm the milk (and ale, if using) and butter to blood heat, add the yeast and milk to the flour and mix to a dough. Knead on a lightly floured surface for 5–10 minutes until the dough is smooth and elastic, adding a little more flour if necessary. Knead in the dried fruit.

Put the dough back into the cleaned bowl, cover with greased plastic wrap and leave in a warm place for 1¹/₂–2 hours until risen and doubled in bulk.

Knock back the dough, then divide into 10 equal pieces. Shape into buns and arrange on a lightly floured baking tray. Cover again and leave in a warm place to rise again for about 15 minutes.

Meanwhile, pre-heat the oven to gas mark 6, 400°F (200°C).

Bake on the top shelf for 15–20 minutes. While the buns are baking, prepare a sugar glaze. Simmer the sugar in a little water until thick, then stir in the rosewater; this isn't strictly necessary but adds that authentic seventeenth-century touch, giving a fragrant perfume to the syrup. Brush the buns with the glaze as they come out of the oven. Serve hot, spread with butter.

Date and walnut loaf

Makes 2 loaves

Serve this simply as a side dish to a cup of tea, or more adventurously with a wedge of English cheese. If you store it in an airtight container it will improve with age.

Kevin Woodford

8 oz (225 g) margarine
4 oz (100 g) sugar
8 oz (225 g) dates
2 oz (50 g) walnut pieces
1 lb (450 g) plain flour
1½ teaspoons bicarbonate of soda
1 teaspoon ground ginger
¼ teaspoon salt

Place the margarine, sugar, 5 fl oz (150 ml) water and the dates in a large saucepan. Bring to the boil then reduce the heat to a simmer and cook for 10 minutes, stirring constantly. Set aside to cool.

Pre-heat the oven to gas mark 2, 300°F (150°C). Lightly grease 2 × 2 lb (900 g) loaf tins. Add the walnuts, flour, bicarbonate of soda, ginger and salt to the date mixture and stir well to mix. Spoon the batter into the 2 tins. Bake for 1½ hours or until a toothpick inserted in the centre comes out clean. Cool in the tins for 10 minutes, then turn out onto a wire rack. Serve warm or at room temperature.

Malt loaf

The flavour of this sticky, rich malt loaf improves with keeping so plan for this before you cut the first slice.

Shirley Goode

2 oz (50 g) sultanas
5 oz (150 g) natural yoghurt
8 oz (225 g) plain wholemeal flour
1 teaspoon bicarbonate of soda
Pinch of salt
3 dessertspoons malt drinking powder
2 dessertspoons black treacle
1 egg, beaten
Clear honey, to glaze

Mix the sultanas and yoghurt together and set aside overnight.

Pre-heat the oven to gas mark 5, 375°F (190°C). Lightly grease a 2 lb (1 kg) loaf tin and line with grease-proof paper.

Sift together the flour, bicarbonate of soda, salt and malt drinking powder. Put the treacle into a jug and blend in 2 dessertspoons hot water. Add to the flour mixture with the egg and the sultanas and yoghurt. Stir until well mixed.

Put the malt mixture into the prepared loaf tin and bake for 45 minutes. Cover the top with aluminium foil after 10 minutes to prevent the loaf getting too brown.

Remove the loaf from the tin and place on a wire rack to cool. Brush the top with honey while still hot. When cool, wrap the loaf tightly in foil and keep at least 1 day before eating.

Walnut thins

Makes about 30

These thin, nutty biscuits go well with ice-creams, fruit fools or salads and creamy mousses. They melt in the mouth and are thoroughly irresistible. If you don't have any walnuts, try hazelnuts or almonds instead.

Sophie Grigson

2 oz (50 g) plain flour
Pinch of salt
2 oz (50 g) caster sugar
1 oz (25 g) walnut pieces, finely chopped
1¹/₂ oz (40 g) butter, melted

Sift the flour with the salt into a medium-sized mixing bowl and mix in the sugar and walnuts. Stir the butter into the dry ingredients, mixing thoroughly to form a soft dough.

Mould the dough into a sausage shape about 2 in (5 cm) thick on a sheet of greaseproof paper. Roll up in the paper and chill until firm (at least 30 minutes).

Pre-heat the oven to gas mark 4, 350°F (180°C).

Slice the dough as thinly as possible and lay on an ungreased baking tray, leaving a good 1 in (2.5 cm) gap between. Bake for 5 minutes until lightly browned at the edges. Remove quickly from the oven and leave to cool for at least 5 minutes before attempting to move – by then they should have become crisp. Store in an air-tight container.

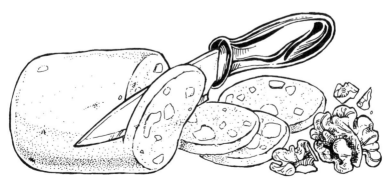

Bernadine's bargain bread

Makes 2 loaves

This recipe gives you two loaves for 55p, they only need one rising and they taste terrific. What more could one ask for?

Bernadine Lawrence, London

1¹/₂ pints (870 ml) water
1 dessertspoon sugar
6 teaspoons dried yeast
3 lb (1.5 kg) wholemeal flour
2 teaspoons salt

Pre-heat the oven to its lowest setting to warm up.

Warm the water until it is hand-hot (about 110°F). Dissolve the sugar in 5 fl oz (150 ml) of the water, add the yeast and leave in a warm room to froth for about 10 minutes.

Sift the flour into a large bowl with the salt. When the yeast has fully dissolved and is very frothy, pour the yeast mixture onto the flour. Add the rest of the warm water gradually and knead the liquid into the flour. Knead well for 10–15 minutes until the dough is smooth and elastic and not too sticky. Add a little more flour if necessary. Halve the dough and place each half in a greased and floured 1¹/₂ lb (750 g) loaf tin.

Switch off the oven, put the tins in and let the dough rise in the oven until it fills the tins completely – check after about 30 minutes.

Bake the bread at gas mark 6, 400°F (200°C) for about 40 minutes until brown on top.

Flat Italian onion bread

Makes one 14 in (35 cm) round loaf

A very substantial bread which is excellent served warm with a winter casserole, soup or some cheese. If you don't like onions, you can easily adapt this recipe, using garlic and herbs instead.

Lesley Waters

2 oz (50 g) fresh yeast, or 1 oz (25 g) dried plus a pinch of sugar
1 lb (450 g) plain flour
1 lb (450 g) granary or wholemeal flour
1 tablespoon salt
10 fl oz (300 ml) sunflower oil
1 oz (25 g) butter
2 large onions, sliced
Freshly ground black pepper
Coarse sea salt (optional)

Blend the fresh yeast with 6 table-spoons warm water until dissolved. If using dried yeast, dissolve in 6 table-spoons warm water with a pinch of sugar and set aside for 10–15 minutes until frothy.

Sift both flours with the salt into a large bowl. Add the oil and the yeast with 12 fl oz (350 ml) warm water and mix together. Add to the flours and stir until a soft dough is achieved. (If the dough is too sloppy, add a little extra flour when kneading. If on the other hand it is too dry, add a little extra water in the mixing.) Knead the dough for 10 minutes or until smooth and elastic. Put the dough back into the cleaned bowl, cover with greased plastic wrap and leave in a warm place about 1½ hours until risen and doubled in size.

Meanwhile, melt the butter in a frying-pan. Add the onions and fry until softened and lightly coloured. Season to taste with pepper and set aside to cool.

Knock back the dough until it is flat. Put the onions in the centre and enclose with the dough, kneading again for about 5 minutes or until the onions are mixed in and the dough is firm and smooth. Place the dough on a greased baking tray and roll it out to a 14 in (35 cm) round. Slash the surface of the dough in a lattice fashion, sprinkle with a little coarse salt, if using, and cover again with a greased plastic wrap. Place in a warm place to rise again for 10 minutes.

Pre-heat the oven to gas mark 6, 400°F (200°C). Dust the top of the bread with a little flour and bake in the top of the oven for 1 hour. The loaf is baked when it sounds hollow if tapped on the bottom. It should be nicely browned with a crisp crust. Cool on a wire rack.

Oatcakes

Makes 12

Eaten with cheese or honey these are really lovely. You can either use fine oatmeal or whizz quick-cooking porridge oats in a blender or food processor to make your own oat flour.

As these cook so quickly, you can use the residual heat left when the oven has just been turned out after cooking something else. This works best, however, with an electric oven that has been set at 375°F (190°C) or higher.

Shirley Goode

8 oz (225 g) fine oatmeal or oat flour
Pinch of salt
1½ oz (40 g) bacon fat or lard, melted

Pre-heat the oven to gas mark 6, 400°F (200°C).

Mix together the oatmeal and salt, then stir in the melted fat with a very small amount of hot water to bind. Knead the mixture gently and turn out onto a work surface sprinkled with oatmeal.

Thinly roll out the dough and cut into rounds or triangles. Place on a greased baking tray and bake for 5–10 minutes until crisp. Cool on a wire rack. Store in an air-tight container.

Preserves

Apple jam

Makes 2 lb (900 g)

Use this jam as a filling for pies, cakes and tarts. It can also be added to sauces, soups and casseroles to give extra body and flavour, as well as making a delicious spread.

Lesley Waters

2 oz (50 g) butter
Grated zest and juice
  of 1 lemon
2 large bay leaves
2 oz (50 g) light brown
  sugar
4 lb (1.75 kg) unpeeled
  cooking apples,
  cored and cut into
  large chunks

Melt the butter in a large saucepan, then add the lemon zest and juice, bay leaves and brown sugar. Stir to-gether and add the apples.
   Cover and cook gently, stirring occasionally, until soft, then cook over a high heat about 5 minutes until the apple mixture is of dropping consistency. Finish the jam by pushing the mixture through a sieve for a rich, smooth purée, or leave for a coarse textured jam. Spoon into warm jars and cover. Store in the refrigerator.

Mixed berry low-sugar jam

Makes 1 lb (450 g)

A real old-fashioned tasting jam, bursting with fresh fruit flavour yet with half the sugar of a traditional jam. Because it has less sugar it doesn't keep so well, so make in small quantities and store in the fridge for 2–3 weeks only.

Gill MacLennan

1 lb (450 g) mixed fruit
  such as raspberries,
  strawberries and red-
  and blackcurrants
6 oz (175 g) sugar

Hull raspberries and strawberries, and top and tail the currants. Place the currants in a pan with 1 tablespoon water and simmer for 5 minutes until the fruit is tender. Add the rasp-berries and strawberries and simmer for a further 5 minutes until they sof-ten. Remove the pan from the heat.

Stir in the sugar until it dissolves.
Return to the heat and boil rapidly,
stirring occasionally, for 10 minutes or
until the setting point is reached.
Spoon into warm jars, cover and
refrigerate.

Watermelon and orange preserve

Makes 3 lb (1.5 kg)

*This preserve makes a delightful summer
jam which can be used not only as a
spread, but to flavour creams, or to serve
(instead of syrup) with hot buttered
pancakes.*

Lesley Waters

**2 lb (1 kg) watermelon,
de-seeded and cut
into chunks
2¹/₂ lb (1 kg 225 g) sugar
Juice of 1 lemon
Grated zest of 3
oranges
14 large oranges,
skinned with all pips
removed and
quartered**

Put the watermelon, 1¹/₂ lb (750 g)
sugar and lemon juice into a large
saucepan and cook very slowly for
1 hour, stirring occasionally.

Meanwhile, prepare the orange
jam. Place the orange zest and
oranges in a large saucepan with 10 fl
oz (300 ml) water and the remaining
sugar. Bring to the boil and boil gently
for 1 hour.

When the two jams are ready, mix
them together and boil for a further 5
minutes. Spoon into clean, warm and
dry jam jars and set aside to cool
completely. When cold, place small
rounds of waxed or greaseproof paper
on top and cover with larger rounds
of greaseproof paper or cellophane.
Securely fasten with string or a rubber
band. Store in a cool, dark place.

Rowan and apple jelly

Makes 4–6 small pots

Nothing beats a home-made jelly, especially those made with fruit that is free for the picking. Rowan berries are the bright red berries hanging like clusters of forbidden fruit on the Mountain Ash or Rowan tree in autumn. They make a beautiful, jewel-bright ruby jelly, which is excellent with meats of all kinds, especially game. Pick the berries on a bright sunny day as soon as they are ripe and before the frost (or birds) get to them.

Lynda Brown

1¹/₂–2 lb (750 g–1 kg) rowan berries, removed from stalks
12 oz–1 lb (350–450 g) cooking or crab apples (ie half the weight of rowan berries), unpeeled, uncored and coarsely chopped
2 lb 4 oz–3 lb (1–1.5 kg) sugar

Place the berries and apples in a large heavy based saucepan with enough water to cover by a depth of 2 in (5 cm), then simmer 20–30 minutes, until soft, mashing the fruit occasionally. Strain the pulp through a sieve and then pass the juice through muslin. Alternatively, strain the lot through a jelly bag, leaving it to drip overnight, if necessary, without touching.

Measure the juice and return to the cleaned-out pan. Stir in 1 lb (450 g) sugar for every 1 pint (600 ml) juice and set over a low heat, stirring, until the sugar has dissolved. Increase the heat and boil rapidly until setting point is reached, skimming off any scum as it rises. The setting point is 220–225°F (97–99.5°C) on a sugar thermometer, though the spoon or saucer test is just as reliable: if the last drop will not drop from the spoon, or it forms wrinkles when a few drops are put onto a cold saucer, it is ready. Be careful not to over-boil or the jelly will be 'jammy'. Pour into sterilised jars, seal tightly, label and store in a cool place.

Windfall chutney

Makes 4 lb (1.75 kg)

A good way of using up windfall apples and greenhouse tomatoes, this thick, dark chutney is best left to mature before you eat it. It'll keep for a year. It is good served with a hunk of granary bread and a piece of farmhouse cheese, or some sliced ham and pickled onions.

Gill MacLennan

8 oz (225 g) whole seed-less mandarin oranges, finely chopped with skins
1 lb (450 g) ripe to-matoes, skinned and coarsely chopped
1 lb (450 g) cooking apples, peeled, cored and chopped
1 lb (450 g) large onions, peeled and coarsely chopped
3 garlic cloves, chopped
8 oz (225 g) stoned dates, coarsely chopped
2 teaspoons salt
1 tablespoon ground cloves
1 tablespoon ground coriander
2 pints (1.2 litres) malt vinegar
2 lb (1 kg) dark brown sugar, unrefined if possible
4 oz (100 g) black treacle

Place the oranges, tomatoes, apples, onions, garlic and dates in a large pan with the salt, cloves, coriander and 1 pint (600 ml) of the vinegar. Bring to the boil, reduce the heat and simmer, uncovered, for 1½ hours, stirring occasionally until the mixture is soft and pulpy.

Add the remaining 1 pint (600 ml) vinegar, the sugar and treacle, then simmer a further 15 minutes until the mixture has thickened.

Ladle the chutney into warmed jars and cover with vinegar-proof tops while still hot. Store in a cool dark place for 2–3 months before using.

Somerset chutney

Makes 10 lb (5 kg)

I think this is the most wonderful accompaniment to anything from a 'sausage butty' to a wide wedge of cheese, but especially nice with a meaty pork pie.

You will need plenty of glass jars in order to store this so plan well ahead. Make sure you thoroughly clean and sterilise the jars before you put the chutney in. The jars should be hot when you add the chutney so they don't crack. Also make sure you have a large enough pan to cook the mixture in. If not, you will have to cook it in several batches.

Kevin Woodford

2 lb (1 kg) green tomatoes, coarsely chopped
2 lb (1 kg) onions, chopped
2 lb (1 kg) cooking apples, peeled, cored and sliced
1 lb (450 g) sultanas
1 lb (450 g) raisins
2 lb (1 kg) Barbados sugar
3 garlic cloves, crushed
¹/₂ tablespoon salt
1 oz (25 g) pickling spice
¹/₂ tablespoon cayenne pepper
1¹/₂ pints (900 ml) malt vinegar

Place the tomatoes, onions and apples in a large saucepan with the dried fruit, sugar, garlic, seasoning, spices and top with the vinegar. Bring to the boil and remove any scum that appears, then reduce the heat to a simmer and let it simmer very gently for 1¹/₂–2 hours, occasionally stirring to prevent it sticking to the bottom of the pan. It is ready when nearly all of the vinegar has been absorbed into the fruit and the gap left when you drag a spoon across the mixture does not instantly refill.

Pour the hot chutney into hot, sterilised jars right to the top. Cover with waxed sealing discs and seal with a tight lid immediately. Label and leave for at least 3 months before eating.

Corn relish

Makes 3 lb (1.5 kg)

A very good relish to eat with cold meats, especially chicken and turkey. It keeps well for up to six weeks in the fridge, and can also be frozen.

Shirley Goode

1 lb (450 g) sweet corn kernels, fresh or frozen
5 fl oz (150 ml) white vinegar
5 fl oz (150 ml) cider
6 oz (175 g) red and green peppers, de-seeded and diced
1 small white cabbage, about 8 oz (225 g), very finely chopped
1 large onion, finely sliced
1 tablespoon brown sugar
2 tablespoons plain flour
1 dessertspoon dry mustard
1 dessertspoon salt
1 teaspoon turmeric

Place the corn, vinegar, cider, peppers, cabbage, onion and sugar in a large saucepan. Bring to the boil, reduce heat to a simmer and cook for 15 minutes, stirring occasionally.

Mix together the flour, mustard, salt and turmeric, then stir into the pan of vegetables until it thickens. Cook for a further 5 minutes, stirring often.

Place the relish in a large bowl and cover. When cool, keep in the fridge for 1 day for the flavours to develop. Store in sterilised jars with vinegar-proof lids.

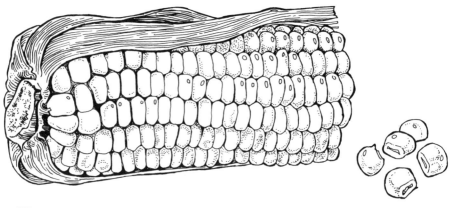

Freezer cucumber pickles

Makes approximately
12 oz (350 g)

This is an American idea. An instant sweet pickle to keep in the freezer, ready to pull out whenever you want to serve with cold meat and salads. By altering the spices, you can make any number of slightly different versions of these crunchy refreshing pickles. Often, I will prepare two different versions, adding half the cucumber mixture to each and freezing in separate containers.

Lynda Brown

1¹/₂–2 cucumbers, scrubbed but not peeled, and thinly sliced
¹/₂ small onion, very thinly sliced
1–2 tablespoons green pepper, finely chopped (optional)
1–2 teaspoons salt
8 tablespoons cider or wine vinegar
1 oz (25 g) sugar
A good pinch of turmeric and celery seeds *or* dill seeds; *or* of celery seeds or dill seeds alone; *or* ¹/₂–1 teaspoon whole grain mustard

Place the cucumber in a bowl with the onion and green pepper if using. Sprinkle over the salt and mix well, then leave the vegetables for a couple of hours for the salt to draw the moisture out.

Tip the vegetables into a sieve and rinse under cold running water, then drain well. Mix the vinegar and sugar together, stirring until the sugar has dissolved, then add a good pinch of the spices you are using. Pour over the cucumber mixture, cover and leave in the refrigerator overnight. Next day, transfer to freezer containers, label and freeze.

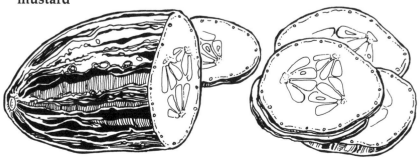

Raspberry vinegar

My mother used to make several bottles of raspberry vinegar each year which we would dilute with hot water for a winter drink or with soda water for a cool refreshing summer cup. A dessertspoonful drunk neat was, as I remember, always given for a sore throat – and very soothing it was, too.

Shirley Goode

1 lb (450 g) ripe raspberries
1 pint (600 ml) white vinegar
Sugar

Place the fruit in a large bowl and press gently with a wooden spoon to release juices. Add the vinegar, cover with a clean cloth and set aside for 1 week, pressing the fruit and giving it a good stir every day.

After 7 days, strain the juice through muslin. Measure and add 1 lb (450 g) sugar to each 1 pint (600 ml) juice. Heat gently until the sugar dissolves, then bring to a fast boil, skimming the surface as necessary. Boil 10–15 minutes or until thick and syrupy, then remove from heat and cool. Store in sterilised bottles with screwcap tops. I use empty vinegar bottles.

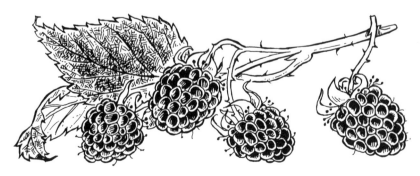

# Index